CAREER TRANSITIONS

A Journey of Survival & Growth

Cara DiMarco
Lane Community College

GORSUCH SCARISBRICK, PUBLISHERS
An imprint of PRENTICE HALL
Upper Saddle River, New Jersey 07458

Library of Congress Cataloging-in-Publication Data

DiMarco, Cara.
    Career transitions : a journey of survival and growth /
Cara DiMarco.
        p.   cm.
    Includes bibliographical references and index.
    ISBN 0-89787-829-9 (alk. paper)
    1. Career changes. 2. Vocational guidance. I. Title.
HF5384.D55   1997
650.14—dc21   96-37862
                                                                                    CIP

Publisher:	Gay L. Pauley
Editor:	Shari Jo Hehr
Developmental Editor:	Katie E. Bradford
Production Editor:	Ann Waggoner Aken
Cover Design:	Don Giannatti
Typesetting:	Andrea Reider

Printed in the United States of America.

10 9 8 7 6 5 4 3 2

ISBN 0-13-776915-6

Prentice-Hall International (UK) Limited, *London*
Prentice-Hall of Australia Pty. Limited, *Sydney*
Prentice-Hall Canada Inc., *Toronto*
Prentice-Hall Hispanoamericana, S.A., *Mexico*
Prentice-Hall of India Private Limited, *New Delhi*
Prentice-Hall of Japan, Inc., *Tokyo*
Simon & Schuster Asia Pte. Ltd., *Singapore*
Editora Prentice-Hall do Brasil, Ltda., *Rio de Janeiro*

Brief Contents

For a complete table of contents, see p. v.

Contents

7   FINDING YOUR SPARK
. . . .
Personal Passion and Life Purpose   **91**

8   MAKING YOUR MARK
. . . .
Creating a Personal Success Definition   **105**

9   HEADS OR TAILS
. . . .
Making Smart Decisions   **127**

Preface

Career Transitions: A Journey of Survival and Growth is written for adults in the midst of career and life changes. Changing careers is a challenging process, and adults engaged in this process face both survival and growth needs. They require support and a clear, yet individualized, path to follow.

Career Transitions is designed to offer support and guidance throughout the career transition process. It provides a model, which I call the "On Target model," for gathering and recording information based on eight dimensions: values, skills, personal characteristics, financial resources, energy resources, personal passion and life goals, success definition, and special concerns. Career options are then explored in terms of these same dimensions: for each dimension readers are able to evaluate whether a career option is a "very good fit," an "adequate fit," or an "undesirable fit."

The book includes examples of elements for each of the eight dimensions and blank copies of the model for readers' use as they gather information about themselves and their possible careers. At the end of each chapter is a "Focus" section, providing readers with an opportunity to personalize the insight gained from that chapter; record leads, thoughts, and ideas to pursue; and answer questions to increase their understanding of the material. Chapters 3 through 8 also include examples of informational interviewing questions to use later in the career exploration process.

In addition to helping readers explore personal and career information, *Career Transitions* provides a framework for making clear decisions based on this information. Readers are able to determine whether they are on a survival-based or growth-based career path, helping them to sort information accordingly and make decisions appropriate to their personal circumstances.

This book acknowledges the reality faced by those engaged in career and life transitions, which are rarely easy. It engages readers in a process that is systematic and encouraging. It helps readers work through the confusion, face the challenges, and make career choices that are right for them.

Acknowledgments

My sincere thanks to the following people, who read and reviewed all or part of the manuscript and provided valuable suggestions and feedback: Nina Stensby-Hurst, James Madison University; Carole Dobbie,

College of Du Page; Marilyn Glenn, Fresno City College; Adrienne Pierre-Charles, De Anza College; Donna Fung, De Anza College; Gloria Davenport, Rancho Santiago College; Dennis Sadler, Rancho Santiago College; Joan Vintle, Lorain County Community College; Linda Scharf, Miami Dade Community College; and Elbert Butler, Monroe Community College.

Cara DiMarco

1

TAKING AIM
Focusing on the On Target Model

THIS BOOK IS WRITTEN FOR...

This book is written for anyone contemplating a career change for any number of reasons: physical injury, divorce, geographical relocation, impending loss of employment, or a growing desire for greater personal and career fulfillment.

Career change has often been construed as moving from one paid position to another. I like to broaden that definition to include making a significant shift in the nature of work activities in everyday life.

A career shift can encompass changing your job environment, making a transition from working within the home to working outside the home, or moving from an unpaid volunteer situation to one for which you are financially compensated. It can also encompass moving your office from an arena outside the home to within the home or starting your own small business. For example, a career change occurs when someone who has retired reenters the work force or when someone's job ceases to exist.

Often, people say, "Well, how can I be changing careers—I haven't worked a real job since I left high school?" For the purpose of this book, view career change as a refocus or a shifting of what you're doing with the work portion of your day, rather than as work you have done that others would consider a "career."

HOW TO USE THE ON TARGET MODEL

The On Target model has eight dimensions that compose a circle with three concentric rings, or sections (see Figure 1.1). Each dimension represents a crucial area of information to gather and consider when

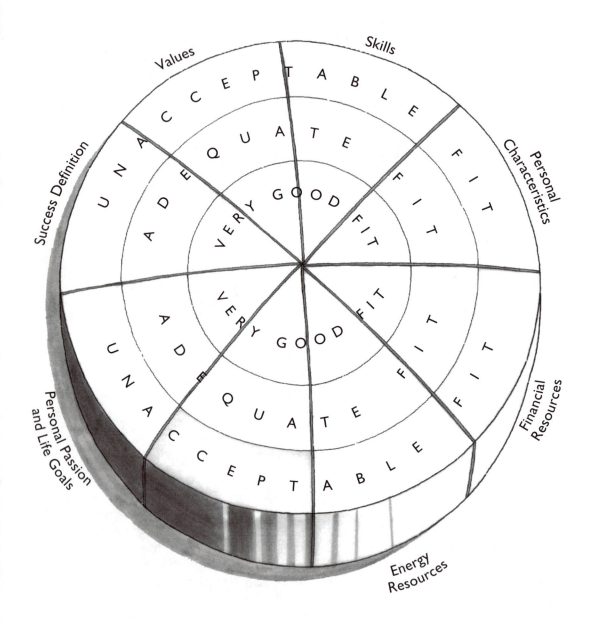

FIGURE 1.1   The On Target model.

weighing job and career options. As you read through these chapters, you will have the opportunity to personalize each dimension by uncovering your values, skills, resources, personal characteristics, life goals, and definition of personal success.

The three concentric rings, or sections, correspond to various levels of fit or match between, for example, your values and the values expressed or embodied in a particular career. The innermost section contains the values that are most important to you, the middle section contains other values that would make a job acceptable to you, and the outermost section contains values that would make a job unacceptable to you.

Once you have collected this information for each dimension, you can then fill in the corresponding sections of the On Target model in Chapter 8. With your completed On Target model in hand, you can start to compare the information you gathered about yourself with the career information that you collected. You can ask yourself if the skills required for a certain job are a very good fit or an unacceptable fit with the skills you want to use in a job.

Careers that cluster around the very good fit section of the model for all eight dimensions will be a better fit with your personal preferences, characteristics, and resources, increasing the likelihood that you will be satisfied with your career choice. In addition, you can rank the importance of each dimension or wedge to make certain that your most important dimensions match your career choice. This will be discussed in Chapter 10.

The questions in the box below help you understand what each wedge is all about. This information will be repeated in Chapter 2, when you begin filling in your own On Target model. For now, simply compare the questions for each of the eight wedges with the sample completed model in Figure 1.2.

Fork in the Road: Growth vs. Survival

As you use the On Target model, you'll see that a helpful tool is to label one model "growth and enrichment" and another "safety and survival." Doing so enables you to sort information into two separate decision-making forks in the road. In Chapter 9, I'll talk in depth about making smart decisions. The decision-making process is often difficult because people mix their survival needs with their growth desires when gathering information and trying to make choices. Some information points toward choices that would be growth enducing and enriching, such as pursuing a developing talent that you feel passionate about, and some information points to choices that ensure safety and survival needs, such as paying the rent and utility bills.

The Eight Wedges of the On Target Model

VALUES
➤ What values do you or do you not want to express in a career?

SKILLS
➤ What skills do you most want to use or not use in your work?

PERSONAL CHARACTERISTICS
➤ Which personal characteristics or strengths would you like to use regularly in your work? Which ones would you like to avoid using?

FINANCIAL RESOURCES
➤ What financial resources do you need your work to provide?

ENERGY RESOURCES
➤ Which time and energy resources (emotional, physical) do you want to expend in your work? Which do you want to reserve for your personal life?

UNTITLED
(SPECIAL CONCERNS)
➤ Skip this wedge for now. In Figure 1.2 the untitled wedge has been labeled "Geographic Preference" and filled in with examples. Information on how to pick a topic for your untitled wedge will be provided in Chapter 6.

PERSONAL PASSION
AND LIFE GOALS
➤ Which life goals and personal passions (activities you love that motivate and energize you) do you want your work to include or lead to?

SUCCESS DEFINITION
➤ What would need to be present in your work for you to feel personally successful?

If you choose to fill out a survival model, there are several things to consider. First, be aware that what may constitute survival for another person may seem like far more or far less than what you need to survive. Definitions of survival vary from person to person and depend on your situation, current level of resources, and individual definition of survival. Because your definition of survival is based on your personal circumstances, don't be concerned if your survival model looks substantially different than someone else's. There is no wrong way to fill out your model, as long as you make certain that it accurately represents what is true for you.

Second, many people find that their filled-in survival model contains far less information than their growth model simply because they are only dealing with the minimal, essential details and needs of their situation. In addition, you may find that you write most of your information in the adequate fit ring, with a few things in the unacceptable fit ring, focusing your energy on what is adequate or tolerable, rather than on what is ideal for you. See Figure 1.3 for an example of a completed On Target Survival model.

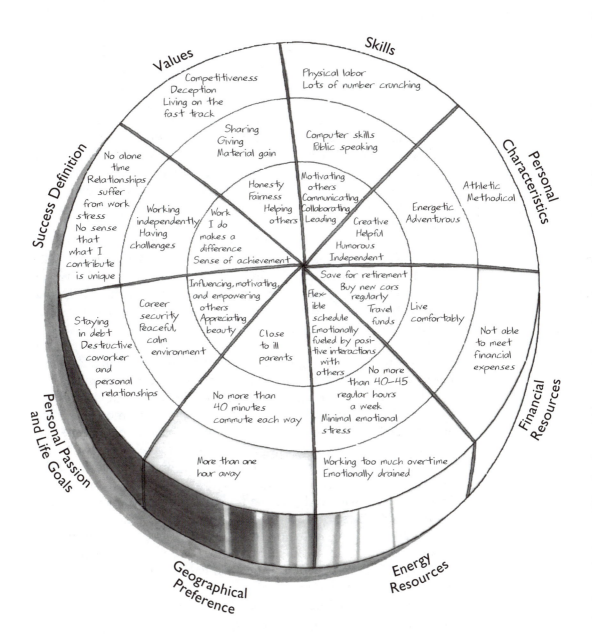

FIGURE 1.2 Example of a completed On Target *Growth* model.

Third, you may feel that several wedges of the model, such as success definition and personal passion and life goals, do not seem to apply to you while you are in the midst of a survival mode. If that is the case for you, feel free to fill out only the wedges that are pertinent to your survival situation.

Most of us are in positions that somewhat blend both growth and survival concerns, and it's useful and instructive to gather information in both arenas. Even if you're fairly certain that you're operating more in one arena than in the other, gathering and recording this information separately is still important. If you need to make a career choice based on survival and safety concerns, completing some exercises may be difficult because you're thinking, "Well, that's not practical or this doesn't matter because I have to do this other less appealing thing anyway." If, however, you have an On Target model that you're using for growth and enrichment possibilities, you can still record that information and keep it from distracting you during your decision-making process.

Conversely, if your survival needs are basically taken care of regardless of the choices you make and you can pursue growth-related issues, you still might find it useful to fill out an On Target model for survival issues in case your circumstances change. Doing so provides a back-up plan should your finances, health, or personal resources diminish unexpectedly.

In addition, many people find that their survival and growth choices actually fall along the same thematic life path (such as wanting to help others), yet their survival and growth choices may seem like divergent paths because the clear, undiluted growth choices are made so far down the path that it is difficult to remember that they are ultimately related. One way to remember this is to picture the two choices along a timeline, with the majority of the survival choices occurring during the front end of the timeline and the majority of the growth choices occurring later. Naturally, survival choices and growth choices will overlap as the transition from one phase of life to another unfolds (see Figure 1.4). Also, some people may experience several cycles of survival and growth. For example, a person may be in survival mode as a college student, then in growth mode while working in her chosen career, and then back in survival mode when her elderly parents require full-time care. By recognizing where you are along your own timeline, you can better gauge the kinds of choices you need to make in the near future.

HOW TO GET THE MOST OUT OF THIS BOOK

Many of you will change careers more than once, and I'd like to encourage you to come back to this book whenever you are in the

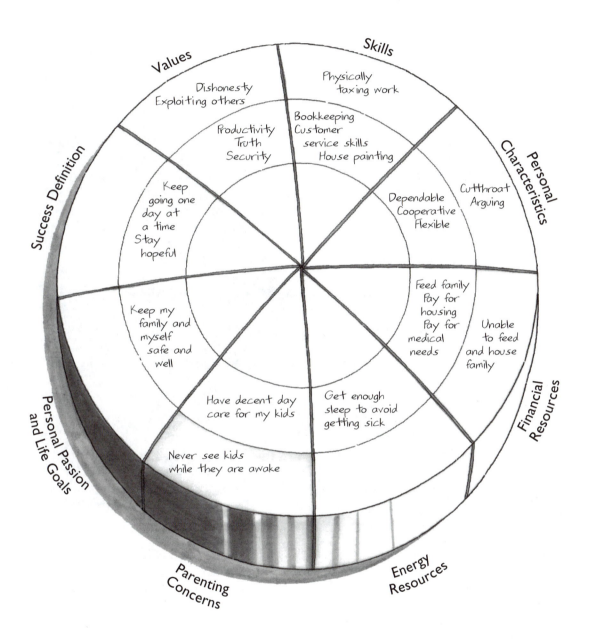

FIGURE 1.3 Example of a completed On Target *Survival* model.

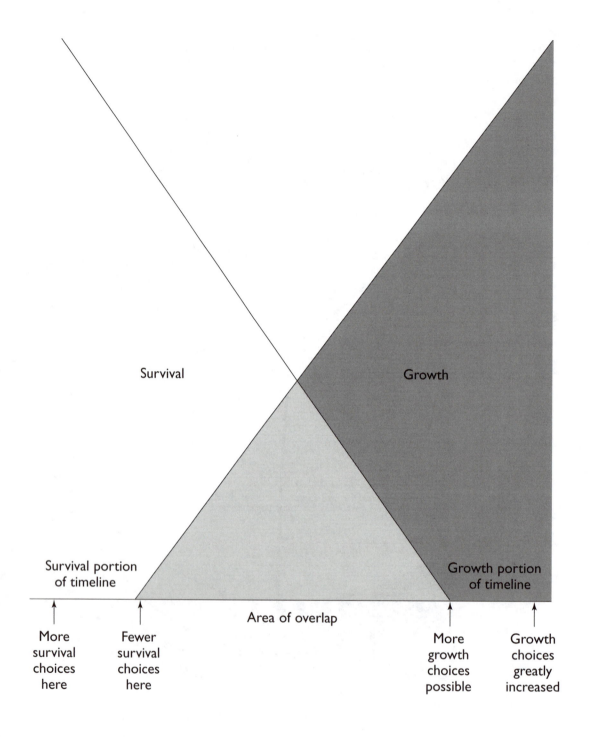

FIGURE 1.4   A timeline showing overlap during transition phases.

midst of a career change. This information is designed to present a clear model that you can apply and use throughout all your career changes. As you work through each section of the On Target model, you will learn a process that you can rely on to help you move through career changes more smoothly and efficiently.

I urge you to read the entire book, even if you think a certain chapter might not be of importance to you, simply because you may discover some useful knowledge embedded in that chapter. If you find information that you are not ready to take action on or examine right now, make some notes on those sections or chapters and give yourself permission to come back and do them later.

It's absolutely legitimate to use the sections that apply at the moment and use others later, as needed, even though this approach may not be as thorough or as ideal as working sequentially through each chapter. One nice thing about looking at this process from a mature adult perspective is that you can trust your judgment about the information you already have and the gaps you want to fill.

If you're not using this book as part of a workshop or a class, I encourage you to visit your local community college or college career center. Most colleges have career centers that can provide a substantial amount of nationally available resources. By exploring them, you can deepen your understanding of certain topics or gain additional input in the areas where you need more information to make decisions.

You'll get the most out of this book if you read each chapter and gather the information you need or draw from your existing knowledge and use the On Target model to consolidate your findings. I encourage you to make several photocopies of the blank On Target model for your current use and to keep a copy in the book as your master copy for future use.

Many of us have made haphazard career choices in the past, "choosing" our career because it seemed like the right thing to do, someone we admired was in that field, or someone we knew could get us a job. Instead of careful consideration, some of us closed our eyes and made our choices by throwing a decision-making dart at an array of choices. The On Target model is designed to make that often blind and scattered process systematic, deliberate, successful and enjoyable—to align your career selection with the rest of your life. With your effort and involvement and with the structured focus of this model, you can be on your way to a career choice that is right on target.

2

CAREER TRANSITIONS
Putting the Process in Perspective

You will face numerous transitions during your life. These may include marriage, a new job, the loss of a job, childbirth, a return to school, divorce, a loss of health, an empty nest, the death of a loved one, relocation, and an endless variety of personal failures and successes that can create the need for a new career direction.

EXPLORING LIFE CHANGES AND NEW CAREER DIRECTIONS

Despite the variety among the transitions that may lead you into a career-change process, certain commonalities exist. All career transitions bring loss—of what was familiar and known, of certainty, of opportunities, of personal history, and of what used to be. Sometimes, especially painful transitions will bring a lost sense of yourself, a loss of perspective, and a loss of hope.

This lost sense of yourself—of your personal power, of a key piece of your identity—can cause you to doubt yourself, to wonder about your ability to see things clearly, and to doubt your capacity to make wise choices about the future. You may feel this way regardless of whether you freely chose your career transition or feel that it is forced on you.

If you freely chose to change careers, you may go through periods when you berate yourself for causing all this avoidable upheaval. You may wonder if you made the right choice, if you can trust your judgment, especially if others did not approve of your choice. You may feel that you have no right to talk about your stress, loss, or fear because you chose the situation. It's essential that you remind yourself that your desire to grow and move toward greater self-fulfillment does not make your stress and pain less valid than the stress and pain of someone who is being forced to do so.

Conversely, if you find yourself in the midst of a career shift as the result of some unforeseen and unwanted circumstance—job market changes, changes in health, a need for additional income, divorce, relocating—you may be experiencing an even greater sense of self-doubt, a sense of having made a series of bad decisions that led to these unwanted circumstances. You may feel that you no longer know what to believe and that life is filled with uncertainty and many unknowns. You may feel frightened, and you may feel the need to make an immediate decision.

Whether your process is voluntary or forced, you may be feeling panicked and pressured. Although it is important to be realistic about your situation and reasonably aware of your time constraints, it's crucial not to overreact. Take time to consider your situation carefully. Can you make decisions at your own pace or do you need to make them quickly because of dire circumstances? Are there certain decisions that you need to make now and others that can wait? If you have the luxury of going at your own pace, can you give yourself a time limit so that you don't gather information forever?

Conversely, if you feel you need to speed the process because of dire circumstances, you might want to talk with people whose judgment you trust or with an objective professional. Discuss how long you have to make a decision so that you're realistic and so that you don't come down too hard on yourself by creating impossible and unnecessary deadlines.

In either case, it's crucial to remind yourself of all that you do know and of all that you do have the ability to impact. You are in a period of life that is rich with possibility and opportunities. With the help of this book and other individuals, you can systematically work toward making the best decision possible for yourself with the information that you have available.

JOBS VERSUS CAREERS

People make a variety of distinctions between a *job* and a *career*. Some people view a job as the tasks you do to earn money and view a career as work that is more a life calling. In this case, the distinction is between *income* and *identity*. Are you working for money, survival, and basic needs, or are you working for personal fulfillment, an expression of your personal identity, or a way to follow your life vision?

Others view a job as a string of work experiences, and view a career as a string of job experiences in a specific profession. Many view a career as encompassing the whole person, the many roles that you play, only one of which concerns your job. My sense of the difference is that a career is what truly fits you, who you fundamentally are—your personal characteristics, attitudes, beliefs, passions, aspirations, values—and that a job is a set of tasks you do to survive and that may or may not fit who you are.

Part of what makes the career-change process such a time of upheaval is that your task is to mesh your personality, who you fundamentally are, with what you do in the world of work. Changing careers creates a time of opportunity, excitement, and fear, because of the many changes that both lead to this process as well as occur during the course of it. Part of this intensity arises because the work you do greatly impacts your sense of identity and how you think of yourself. It's no accident that in new social situations, one of the first questions people ask is, What do you do for a living? It's as though the work you do somehow becomes synonymous with who you are, that your work is the core of your identity.

This correlation between work and identity can become painfully evident when you are in the midst of choosing a new career. Because changing careers is such a reshaping of our identity, both personally and professionally, we can experience a great deal of disruption, confusion, and powerful feelings. With all this also comes the opportunity to look at a variety of issues in your life and to reexamine them. It's also a time when you can make decisions about what still works for you that you want to retain and what no longer works that you may want to discard.

It's a time in which you can reconsider your values, reexamine your skills, look more closely at your sense of identity, and determine where you've grown, what still fits, and what no longer fits. You can reexamine your resources, get back in touch with your sense of passion and life purpose, or question whether your work truly expresses who you are. You may be wanting to redefine what success means to you and to decide which aspects of that definition you'd like present in your life. You may feel that some of your decisions turned out well and that some didn't and that you want to reexamine your decision-making process.

This book is designed to allow you to complete all these tasks, plus provide a structure in which you can systematically accomplish them. Both in reexamining past choices and in choosing a new career direction, you need three basic kinds of information—information about yourself, about particular jobs or careers, and about how to make a well-considered decision. Chapters 3 through 8 will help you unearth and clarify your pertinent personal information as it relates to job choices. The exercises at the end of each chapter will encourage you to seek information about possible career options so that you gradually determine how your personal and career information mesh. Chapter 9 will help you focus on your decision making and introduces a strategy for clear decision making. Finally, Chapter 10 will assist you in pulling all the information together in a usable form. Before we launch into this process, however, it's critical to address how to best cope with the strong feelings of loss, grief, and fear that can emerge in the midst of changing careers.

COPING WELL WITH LOSS, GRIEF, AND FEAR

Loss, grief, and fear are emotions that are guaranteed to come up for anyone in the life-change process. Even if the change feels positive, is chosen, and looked forward to with excitement and enthusiasm, there will still be moments of grieving for the old ways of being in the world, for the old habits, and for the loss of what was familiar.

Change can be hard even if it is chosen and positive, because others in our lives sometimes don't have the patience to support our feelings of loss, grief, and fear. Because they feel that we chose the change, their attitude is that this is something exciting and fun and that we should be happy about it. Well, in every new growth step, in every change, there is loss and grief. We grieve what was familiar, safe, predictable, and known, even if it wasn't positive. We grieve the person we were in that job, in that work environment, and with those coworkers, because even if we welcome the change, we still will never be exactly that person again. Acknowledging that up-front and throughout the information-gathering process is important.

You may find that grief and fear surface without warning, just when you are making headway. Many people find that even if they think they're past their grief, it reappears once they start to consider their options. This occurs because every time we consider a new option, we are also considering its flip side: By making this choice, what am I potentially losing and giving up and how might I regret that in the future? This is usually when fears, worries, and concerns emerge about what could go wrong if we choose incorrectly.

One way to avoid being immobilized by those feelings is to make a list of all your fears, worries, and concerns. Give yourself permission to write all those feelings down on paper, and don't censor yourself by saying, "That's too stupid to be worried about—I can't write that down." It's essential that you start recording, and thus in a sense containing, your worries and fears on paper where it's easier to see them clearly. It's much easier to let something go when it's written down than when it keeps rolling around in the back of your brain. It's also easier to argue with and refute or quiet fears and concerns when they're in black and white in front of you. List at least the first 20 that come to mind, and you can make a longer list if you wish.

Your fears, worries, and concerns list:

1.

2.

3.

4.

5.

6.

7.

8.

9.

10.

11.

12.

13.

14.

15.

16.

17.

18.

19.

20.

After you've compiled your list, look at what themes run through it. For example, are you worried about people's reactions to your changes and the impact it may have on them? Are you worried about losing relationships or resources? Are your losses and fears similar or different? Make a note of any recurring themes; we will return to this list toward the end of the book. You may find that you'll also want to return to this list after you've worked through Chapter 8, in which you'll have the opportunity to look at whether any of your fears are creating a barrier to your vision of success for yourself.

While you're dealing with loss, grief, and fear, you may simultaneously need to be out in the world working on skill acquisition or searching for a job. Trying to work on your next steps—information gathering, job interviewing—while feeling very sad and not especially motivated can be extremely challenging. How do you keep going under these circumstances? One way to push yourself through these hard times is to limit your tasks to those that are essential and to tackle everything else when you feel more emotionally resilient.

Another challenge you may encounter during this time is how to keep your feelings from immobilizing you, yet also how to avoid stuffing, or repressing, your feelings. You may experience so many feelings that you start to feel swamped, overwhelmed, and emotionally pulled down by them. You may reach a point where it's hard to think clearly and function in even the most basic ways out in the world. You may also feel that the faucet of your feelings is difficult to turn off once it's on. It may seem that your only two options are to have the faucet completely open or completely shut. The result is that you're either drowning in your feelings or completely holding them all back.

A third option is possible. For most people, it's possible to be in touch with your feelings and still accomplish what you need in your career-change process. One way to do this is to alternate when you need to be functional and productive with when you need to allow your feelings to surface.

Some people designate home as a "feeling zone" and give themselves permission to feel whatever they need to feel once they walk through the front door. When they need to go to a job interview or engage in another aspect of pursuing a new career, they make a conscious decision to operate out of a purely mental, factual head space. Once the task is completed, they allow themselves to feel whatever emotions the situation generated.

One of my friends likes to envision a tiny elevator that runs between her head and her heart. When she is in the midst of her grief and fear and has a task to complete, she pictures herself getting on the elevator at her heart level and pressing the up button. She then counts off 20 floors as she pictures herself moving up into her head. She sees the elevator door open up in her head, and she steps onto what she calls the "thinking floor." She completes the task and then, when it's appropriate, climbs back on the elevator and travels back to her feelings. You may want to experiment with whatever images allow you to best create a way to contain your feelings when necessary.

While you are going through this emotionally intense period, you need a safe place to express all your feelings. That safe place might take the form of a journal, conversations with a trusted friend, or art, dance, or music. If you feel you need objective, outside guidance, seek professional assistance in sorting through your feelings and fears. Find an outlet for your feelings and process them throughout your career search so that they don't get bottled up inside you.

FOCUS ON THE BIG PICTURE

Looking Within

Write as many endings to each sentence as you can.

1. I am changing careers because…

2. When I think of pursuing a new career, I…

3. What I want most out of a new career is…

4. The positive thing about changing careers is…

Wedge Work

You will spend the next six chapters working your way through the eight wedges of the On Target model. Each chapter focuses on one or more wedges, providing information and exercises designed to help you identify key variables to consider and weigh when making a decision.

Figure 2.1 is a blank On Target model, with seven wedges labeled and one untitled. Starting at the top of the model and moving clockwise, the wedges are values, skills, personal characteristics, financial resources, energy resources, untitled (you will fill this in with any special concerns that you'll want to consider), personal passion and life goals, and your success definition. See the box on the next page for the questions that distinguish the eight wedges; this information was introduced in Chapter 1. More detailed definitions of these concepts will be provided as we move through the model.

The Eight Wedges of the On Target Model

VALUES
➤ What values do you or do not want to express in a career?

SKILLS
➤ What skills do you most want to use or not use in your work?

PERSONAL CHARACTERISTICS
➤ Which personal characteristics or strengths would you like to use regularly in your work? Which ones would you like to avoid using?

FINANCIAL RESOURCES
➤ What financial resources do you need your work to provide?

ENERGY RESOURCES
➤ Which time and energy resources (emotional, physical, mental) do you want to expend in your work?

Which do you want to reserve for your personal life?

UNTITLED (SPECIAL CONCERNS)
➤ Skip this wedge for now. We will return to this wedge in Chapter 6.

PERSONAL PASSION
AND LIFE GOALS
➤ Which life goals and personal passions (activities you love that motivate and energize you) do you want your work to include or lead to?

SUCCESS DEFINITION
➤ What would need to be present in your work for you to feel personally successful?

As stated in Chapter 1, the innermost section of each wedge contains the "very good fit" category for whatever the wedge represents. The middle section represents the "adequate fit" category, and the outermost section represents the "unacceptable fit" category. Although the next six chapters will provide ample opportunity for you to fill in your On Target model systematically, make a partial attempt now to identify a few key variables for yourself before you think in depth about each wedge.

As your first response on a multiple-choice test is most often accurate, your first intuitive response can often embody variables that are essential to your future well-being. In this spirit, fill in any key words or variables for any of the sections of the eight wedges. You may find a certain wedge very easy to fill in, while another wedge is a struggle. Don't overly concern yourself—simply complete whatever portions you can.

Many people find it easiest to fill in aspects of the innermost and outermost sections—what they most need their job to contain (the inner circle) and what they most need their job not to contain (outer circle). The middle section often gets filled in more slowly, as these are variables you'd like to see on your job that would enhance or add

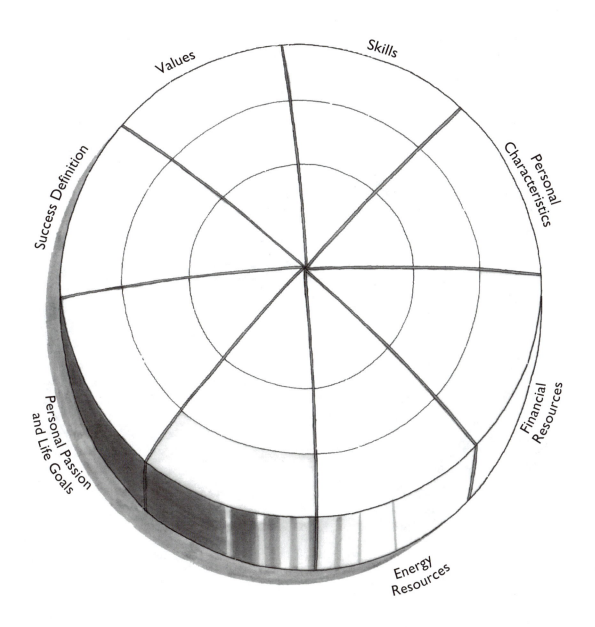

FIGURE 2.1   A blank On Target model.

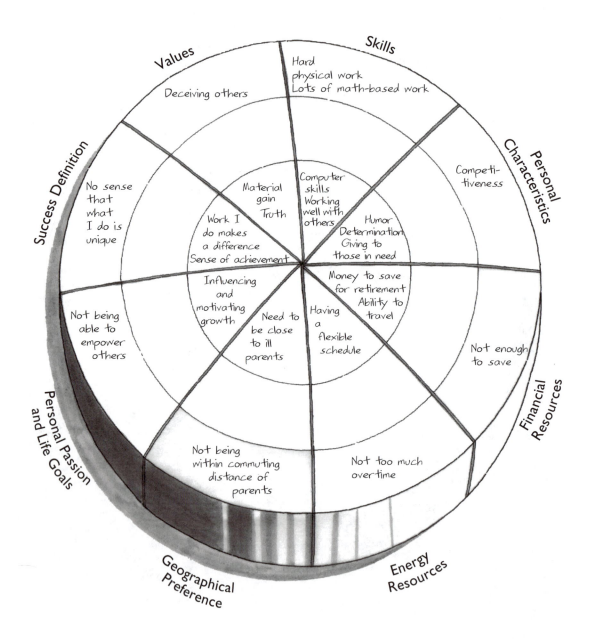

FIGURE 2.2 A best-guess sample model.

to the quality of your life but that are not essential. Figure 2.2 shows a filled-in best-guess sample model.

When you've completed as much of Figure 2.1 as you can, put this model away until you've worked through the entire book. You can then pull out this initial chart and compare it with the model that you've been gradually filling in during the course of the book.

Consider These Questions...

1. What have you learned about your feelings of loss, grief, and fear regarding your career change?

2. What might help you in either learning to cope well or continuing to cope well with these feelings?

3. What resources or individuals might provide you with information on additional coping strategies?

Ideas for Action

Use this space to write down thoughts, leads, ideas, and questions that you want to pursue.

Things to explore now   *Things to explore later*

RECOMMENDED READING

Bridges, William. *Transitions*. New York: Addison-Wesley, 1980.
  Focuses on the three major stages of transitions and describes aspects of endings, the in-between neutral zone, and beginnings.

DiMarco, Cara. *Moving Through Life Transitions with Power and Purpose*. Scottsdale, AZ: Gorsuch Scarisbrick, 1995.
  Provides assistance in dealing with the emotions that transitions often bring, in building new coping skills and behaviors, and in establishing a new sense of direction.

Spencer, Sabina, and John Adams. *Life Changes*. San Luis Obispo, CA: Impact Publishers, 1990.
  Describes a seven-stage mood curve for transitions and includes some brief questions to assist with self-exploration.

3

WHAT MATTERS MOST
Values

Values are the qualities, attitudes, beliefs, traits, and concepts that have special significance or meaning for a person. Your values indicate what is most important to you, what you find desirable and worthwhile.

IDENTIFYING PERSONAL VALUES

An awareness of your most important values can serve as an excellent compass to guide you in making day-to-day choices and decisions. Clarity regarding your most important values can make your career-change process less confusing. Values are:

➤ learned from parents, friends, and significant role models

➤ evolving, changing aspects of your personality

➤ based on individual, personal preferences and priorities

➤ crucial determinants in making good decisions

➤ revealed in your choices, comments, and actions

Especially important as you explore your values as they relate to your career change is the notion that your values evolve over time. Part of the reason your values change is that as you take in and process new information and experiences, you learn, grow, and change. As a result, what you deem important shifts and changes.

Often career dissatisfaction is due in part to values that no longer fit. Sometimes careers can shift to accommodate those value changes and sometimes not. A person can choose a career or a job for reasons that made sense in the past, but that no longer mesh with the person's current values.

For example, advertising was a good match with Darla's values because it was creative, exciting, and provided lots of opportunity to feel powerful. Darla liked the long hours, tension, struggle, and stress. Yet, at some point those experiences and feelings no longer fit with who she had grown to be and with what she had come to value.

Darla doesn't necessarily need to scrap her career choice and leave advertising, but she needs to consider freelancing rather than working a 70-hour week. But if Darla really wants to assist people in their growth process and she doesn't feel she's doing that in her advertising work, she might want to consider working for an agency that specializes in nonprofit advertising or matching advertising consultants with agencies and product lines that assist others in living well. Although Darla has the prerogative to say, "It doesn't fit me anymore, so I'll stop doing it right now," that's not necessarily her only choice.

Identifying and clarifying personal values is important because they are crucial to the matching process and help to assure a good fit between a career and who you are. The old adage of being able to get up in the morning and look at yourself in the mirror also applies to doing work in alignment with your values. Are you doing work that does not directly contradict or destroy what is essentially valuable to you?

Below is a list of some common values:

abundance	education	imagination
accomplishment	engagement	influence
achievement	entertainment	integrity
acquisition	enthusiasm	intimacy
advancement	equality	involvement
adventure	excitement	joy
approval	exercise	knowledge
authenticity	experience	leadership
autonomy	expressiveness	love
beauty	faith	loyalty
belonging	fame	mastery
challenge	family	modesty
change	freedom	nature
comfort	free time	neatness
commitment	friendship	nonconformity
competition	fun	nurturing
consistency	growth	order
control	happiness	patience
cooperation	health	peace
creativity	honesty	persistence
decisiveness	honor	play
determination	hope	pleasure
discipline	humor	power

process	rewards	stimulation
recognition	satisfaction	tenacity
progress	risk-taking	success
prosperity	satisfaction	tenacity
rebellion	security	tradition
recognition	sincerity	travel
religion	space	trust
reputation	spirituality	truth
respect	stability	wisdom

Using this list of values, as well as any other values that you can think of, create a list of what you think your values are right now:

Your List of Values

1.	9.
2.	10.
3.	11.
4.	12.
5.	13.
6.	14.
7.	15.
8.	16.

FAMILY INFLUENCES IN THE SHAPING OF VALUES

Families substantially influence the values that a person acquires. Families shape values in positive and negative ways in terms of what they value, what they do not value, and what they ignore. For example, Carlos grew up in a family that valued hard work and that did not value pleasure and leisure but viewed pleasure and leisure as selfish and immature. Carlos can choose to adopt that exact value system in his adult life and work hard and shun pleasure and leisure; he can choose to partially adopt that value system and work moderately hard and shun leisure; or he can choose a value system that is in direct opposition and work as little as possible and create as much pleasure as possible.

What the family ignores, what never gets mentioned or dealt with also shapes our values. If no one in Carlos's family ever talked about work as a source of pleasure or meaning, perhaps Carlos never got the opportunity to consider it as a value—he never actively chose or actively rejected that value.

You can consciously value or not value something, and you can lack awareness of certain values. We acquire many values from our families before we're capable of much independent thought. It becomes easy to say, "That's just how I look at things," or simply to assume we believe and value the right things. Rarely do we have a chance to question, to ask, "Is that what is most important to me?" Or even more crucial, "Is that what's most important to me at this stage in my life, knowing what I know?"

Reevaluating the values we learned from our family can be frightening because it can feel like betrayal or disloyalty. But time and life situations change, and it would be unrealistic not to take in new information and explore it. You may decide that the value system you were taught as a child fits you well. In that case, you can comfortably continue with the values you currently possess. If for some reason they don't fit, you can think about which values you need to modify or shift in intensity, which you need to put aside altogether, which you need to add and consider. People who put effort and energy into uncovering their values tend to experience greater contentment and to approach others and life with a more positive attitude than those who avoid this task.

1. Make a list of things your family members have said or implied about work, ambition, success, and achievement.
   1.
   2.
   3.
   4.
   5.
   6.
   7.
   8.
   9.
   10.

2. Does your list contain primarily positive or negative things?

3. Circle the things with which you still agree. Choose one thing you disagree with and explain why.

4. Which work-related values were never mentioned or encouraged?

5. Would you like to unlearn any values?

6. Which values are most important to you at this stage of your life?

Sneak Preview of Your Informational Interview

This exercise section is designed to help you create a list of questions that will allow you to gather the career information most pertinent to your preferences and personality. Below are several prepared questions, along with space for you to write any additional questions you may have. At the end of Chapter 9, space is provided in which you can compile a full set of informational interview questions that you will have gathered by working your way from Chapter 3 through Chapter 8.

Read through the following questions, and transfer those most pertinent to you to the informational interview compilation list at the end of Chapter 9. Although you will want to use the tool of informational interviews sparingly and will want to wait to conduct them until you're clear on the specific careers you're considering, you can still explore these questions with other students, family, and friends. Practice asking the people you know some of the informational interview questions about the work they do, and reflect upon what you find appealing and unappealing in their answers. This will provide additional insight into your preferences and how they relate to your career choice.

1. What attitudes, beliefs, and behaviors are valued on the job?
2. What attitudes, beliefs, and behaviors are unacceptable?
3. What do coworkers most value about the work environment?
4. What do coworkers most value about their jobs?
5. How would my values of_____ fit with this job?
   Include your additional personalized questions here:

6.

7.

8.

ATTITUDES TOWARD WORK AND SUCCESS

When you consider the attitudes and values toward work and success demonstrated in your family, what was given priority? Was it money, status, recognition, being of service, helping others, doing work you love, freedom, job security? What was your family's attitude about work? What was emphasized when work was discussed?

Was work considered something to take pleasure in, a potential source of fulfillment? Was it something you just did to pay the bills? Was it considered a necessary evil, part of providing for a family? Was it about becoming cornered or roped into obligations, or was it done for other reasons?

Your family's work values may have radically shaped your response to work. If you don't have a model for work and job success that says that work can be or is a positive experience, exploring your attitudes and viewing work in a different way may be a challenge.

For example, Norman's family believed that if you have a job, you stick with it, regardless of how you feel about it, until you retire. Now Norman is dissatisfied with his job and is considering a career change. He's experiencing a number of intense emotions, including guilt, anxiety, anger, and depression. An internal voice is telling Norman that it's selfish or self-indulgent to leave a perfectly good job and dare to look for something that meets more of his personal values and needs.

I've heard that certain individuals were told, in effect, that "hard work never killed anyone, but resentment did." These individuals struggle with the notion that their dissatisfaction is trivial and shallow and that they should ignore their feelings and values. Perhaps hard work that embodies a person's central values never killed anyone. I'm not so certain that work that's hard and doesn't fit the essence of someone's value system doesn't kill or substantially diminish that person's spirit, passion, and life force over time. You may have to struggle to align your work and your values, but the quality of life gained is worth it.

Remember, 50 years ago jobs rarely ended, in the sense of technology making certain positions obsolete. Although technology was certainly advancing, jobs did not become outmoded at today's pace— for example, manufacturing-based jobs weren't rapidly becoming nonexistent. Unless a plant closed down or someone really had difficulties, jobs rarely ended abruptly, excluding Depression-era times.

Thus, some families believe that people don't lose their jobs or aren't forced into changing careers unless they've really failed. If you grew up with that value system, yet now believe you can leave a job if you're unhappy, you may experience upheaval because you're caught between the old values you grew up with and your current values.

You damage no one by seeking what's important to you. If you are honest and true to yourself about that, you tend to live your life in more congruence. You also tend to be less emotionally disrupted and therefore less disruptive in your relationships with others and, everyone benefits.

Consider also whether your family's view of job success matches yours. In Chapter 8, I'll go into more depth regarding a definition of success. For now, pause and consider whether your family's definition of success matches yours. If not, which values aren't the same? Is it acceptable for you to disagree with your family's values? If it is uncomfortable, can you do something to create more comfort?

A good exercise is to distance yourself from your family's values about work and look at your own personal values—via what you feel strongly about, what you feel is right or wrong—not globally but just for yourself. You'll discover some subtle values that would be more difficult to uncover in other ways. You might discover that you feel it's not healthy for people to do work that they dislike, that life's too short, and that people should do work that means something to them.

You may think it's important for coworkers to cooperate or for people to go out of their way to be kind. Anything you can do to uncover your values will allow you to better evaluate whether certain jobs match your values. Looking at values in this way is different from looking at the skills or personal qualities needed on a job. You can have the necessary skills and qualities to do a job, but if your values don't match the job site values, you can end up feeling miserable. One way to assess this is to talk to people in that field and ask, What do you think the values are of people working in this job or field—what kinds of values do people hold who work here? People may say, "Hey, we work 40 hours a week, and then we're out of here. We don't take anything home." Or they may say, "We value people who put aside their personal needs and pitch in and work an extra 20 hours a week as needed—we value initiative, creativity, and personal sacrifice." All of this is incredibly important information when you're considering career choices; you can compare the prevalent job values with your preferred work values. At the very least, there should be no untenable contradictions. And ideally, you want to experience a reasonable fit, which will add a great deal to your personal satisfaction.

Focus on Values

Looking Within

Write as many endings to each sentence as you can.

1. What I most value...

2. What my family taught me about work…

3. My preferred work environment is…

4. I would like coworkers who…

Wedge Work

Figure 3.1 shows an On Target model with the Values wedge containing some sample values. You can use these samples to get an idea of how filling in these wedges works. Earlier in this chapter, you listed values that are important to you. Now you want to place these values in either the blank Survival Values wedge, as shown in Figure 3.2, or in the Growth Values wedge, as shown in Figure 3.3. To remind yourself of the distinctions between Growth and Survival modes, see Chapter 1.

In the Very Good Fit innermost section of each wedge, list the words that represent key values to have in your work. In the Adequate Fit middle section, list words that reflect values you'd like to express in your work, those that would enhance the quality of your life but that aren't essential. In the Unacceptable Fit outer section, jot down those values that you would not want present in your work, those that would make doing your work nearly impossible.

Once you have a sense that you have gathered all the essential information about yourself onto the enlarged values wedge, you can transfer it to your growth and survival copies of the On Target model in Chapter 8 (Figures 8.4 and 8.5).

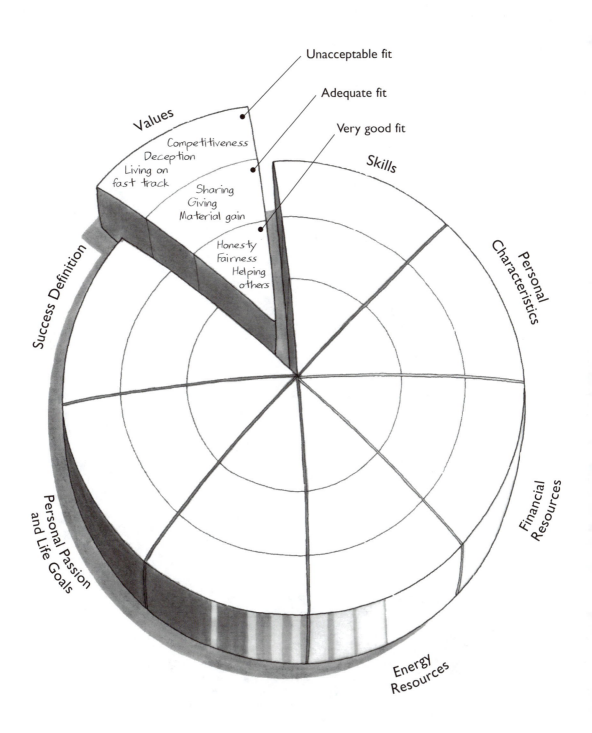

FIGURE 3.1 An On Target model, with the *Values* wedge filled in with sample values.

FIGURE 3.2   A blank *Survival Values* wedge, ready for you to add words that describe your values.

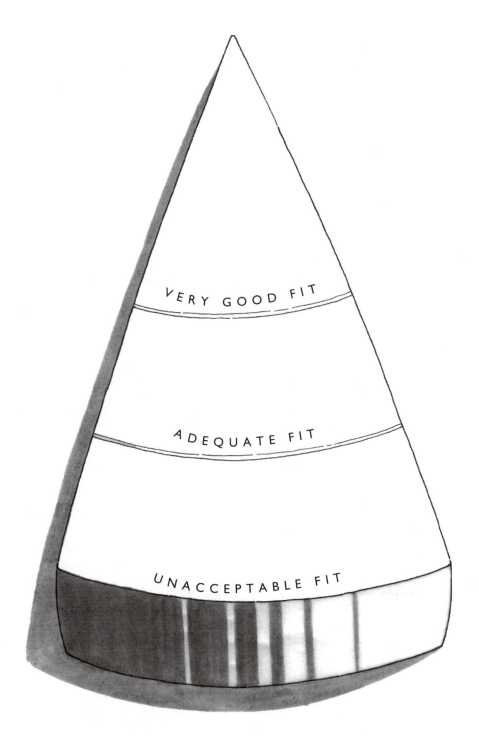

VERY GOOD FIT

ADEQUATE FIT

UNACCEPTABLE FIT

FIGURE 3.3 A blank *Growth Values* wedge, ready for you to add words that describe your values.

Consider These Questions...

1. What have you learned about your most important values?

2. How well have your values fit with your work in the past?

3. What can you do to increase the likelihood of a good fit between your values and the work site values of your next career?

Ideas for Action

Use this space to write down thoughts, leads, ideas, and questions that you want to pursue.

Things to explore now   *Things to explore later*

RECOMMENDED READING

Dean, Amy. *Life Goals.* Carson, CA: Hay House, 1991.

Explores values in different areas of life and provides clarifying exercises and techniques.

Gendler, J. Ruth. *The Book of Qualities.* Berkeley: Turquoise Mountain Publications, 1984.

Presents values and personal qualities as distinct characters in a unique manner that allow people to recognize those that apply in their lives.

Robbins, Anthony. *Awaken the Giant Within.* New York: Fireside, 1991.

Assists readers in identifying what is important to them and to their quality of life and offers strategies and techniques for achieving those things.

4

KNOWING WHAT YOU KNOW
Seeing Your Skills Clearly

What do you do well or have you done well in the past? I'm not talking only about job-related tasks, I'm talking about anything that could be considered a skill that you've done, going back to your earliest memories. These skills could include anything from learning a craft or hobby, fixing or repairing things, or resolving conflicts between others, to more traditional work-related skills. These skills may be associated with activities that you enjoy or dislike.

IDENTIFYING SKILLS YOU CURRENTLY POSSESS

Take a moment and make a list of as many things as you can think of that you do reasonably well. Forget for the moment whether anyone would pay you to perform these skills. Just think about the skills you currently possess and which of them you have performed in the past. Don't limit yourself to only those skills that you can perform very well. Instead, include any skills that you can perform adequately or better.

   Things I can do adequately or better:

1.

2.

3.

4.

5.

6.

7.

8.

9.

10.

11.

12.

13.

14.

15.

16.

17.

18.

19.

20.

Now, put that list aside. Start a second list of skills or abilities that you have wanted to develop but have not. Again, don't think about whether anyone would pay for these skills or whether they would lead to a job. Simply list anything that you ever wanted to do, even if you've since changed your mind and no longer want to learn it. Perhaps at age 10 you wanted to be a lawyer or a teacher or a fire-fighter, and although that no longer appeals to you, the theme related to doing that may still apply. When you complete your second list, put it aside as well. We'll come back to both lists later.

Skills and abilities I have wanted to develop:

1.

2.

3.

4.

5.

6.

7.

8.

9.

10.

11.

12.

13.

14.

15.

16.

17.

18.

19.

20.

As children, we all learned and developed new skills regularly. As we grew, we acquired new physical skills, as well as emotion-based skills, cognitive/mental skills, and social/relating skills. We continually developed new skills at a rate that would seriously challenge us as adults. And yet we learned those skills without feeling especially overwhelmed, simply because we didn't know any differently; it was a natural part of our growth and development.

Sometimes as adults we feel that we can't learn something new, for example, because we're out of practice learning new things. Although you're never too old, you may be out of practice, and the thought of acquiring new skills may be very frightening.

But you improve at what you practice. If you practice dribbling a basketball, you'll get better at dribbling a basketball—you may not ever be the best, but you'll get better at it. If you practice typing, you'll get better at typing. You may not be the world's best typist, but you'll get better at typing. The same applies to running a computer program, operating dental equipment, or reading the stock market page. You will get better at anything you practice.

Some of you may be asking, What about the notion that older people learn skills at a slower rate? Although some data indicates certain skills are easier to learn at a young age, such as mastering a foreign language, the ability to learn most skills is not impaired by a person's age. An individual may find learning new skills more challenging than in previous years because of increased personal responsibilities, because he's out of practice learning anything new, or because her knowledge base is so extensive that making sense out of new information and fitting it into existing frameworks and personal beliefs takes longer.

Returning students often take longer than those who have not interrupted their education to assimilate new information. Rather than accepting and memorizing new information at face value, returning students question the accuracy, relevance, and application of that information and spend time attempting to incorporate that information into their existing pool of knowledge. From the outside, this might look like a slowed-down learning process; in fact, it is deeper, more thorough and all-encompassing.

What should you do if, despite this information, you have concerns about your ability to learn new skills and information? Contact your local community college and enroll in one of the classes designed for adult learners that focuses on study skills, memory enhancement, or identifying learning styles. With the assistance of these courses and a little effort, you can make learning work for you.

DEVELOPING NEW SKILLS

When you think about developing new skills, ask yourself exactly why you're developing these skills: to increase marketability, to increase your self-confidence, for personal enrichment, or to enhance existing skills? A variety of influences may shape your choice of skills to develop. You may feel that you don't especially want to develop a certain skill, but if you do, it will radically increase your marketability. Many individuals that I talk to are not thrilled with the notion of becoming computer literate and have avoided gaining that skill, even though they clearly know that it will increase their job prospects.

You may need or want to develop personal, social, or emotional skills—for example, to acquire self-confidence, to develop public speaking skills to interact and converse better with others, or to be assertive with others. You may need to develop additional skills for personal enrichment and self-growth or to build on skills you currently possess.

Perfectionism can be a barrier to learning new skills. Much of the time, the fear of looking foolish, of not knowing an answer, or not knowing how something is done gets in the way when attempting to learn new skills. Remember, you can't know how to do something if you haven't learned it yet. Everyone has the right to make mistakes, to experiment with learning new things, and to fumble through a new task or activity.

Think about bike riding—a child learning to ride the bike doesn't sit there and say, "Oh, I'm going to look so stupid because I'm going to tip over on my bike." No one expects the child to get on the bike and pedal; if the child could do that, she would already know how to ride the bike. There is no way for the child to learn to ride the bike except to get on it, pedal and tip over until she finds her sense of balance. Although we may dread the tipping over part of learning new skills, it is an essential component of the process.

So how do we get over our dread of the fumbling part of the learning process? One way is to alter the self-defeating language that most of us use when we fear the challenges we encounter. How can you tell if you fear or face challenges? A baseball player in the outfield fears the challenge when he thinks, "Don't hit it to me; I'll blow it." He faces the challenge when he thinks, "Hit it to me; I want to make the play." You can apply the same principle to being called upon in class or to a variety of other situations.

You move from fearing challenges to facing them when you change "I can't learn this skill" to "I haven't learned it yet." Saying "I can't" implies, "Well, it's just too hard to do; it's just not possible." René is trying to learn a computer program, and she keeps struggling and getting stuck in the learning process. René has a couple of choices: She can sit there, look at the computer, bang her head on the table, and say, "I can't learn this. It's impossible. It's too hard for me." Or she can sit there and say, "I'm really frustrated. I'm not enjoying this. I haven't learned how to do this yet, and I'm going to, even if it takes longer than I'd like."

Notice the difference in those two attitudes. Although both attitudes acknowledge René's feelings, the first implies defeat and hopelessness; the second conveys tenacity and a can-do approach. By cultivating this can-do attitude, you motivate yourself, you have a positive outlook, and you increase self-confidence as you work at learning new skills.

Make a list of all the "I can'ts" that potentially limit what you perceive yourself as being able to do as it relates to possible careers.

My "I Can't" List:

1.

2.

3.

4.

5.

6.

7.

8.

9.

10.

11.

12.

13.

14.

15.

16.

17.

18.

19.

20.

Now, rewrite each "I can't" into an "I haven't yet _____, and I'm going to." Even though this may seem like a simple rewording, you'll be surprised at how your attitude toward challenge gradually begins to shift if you consistently reframe your "I can't" into "I haven't yet."

Another way we diminish our abilities and potential is through our use of labels. Labels can focus on our inabilities and can judge our personal characteristics; for example, you can be labeled "too clumsy" or "too quiet." Learn to let go of old limiting labels; they damage your self-esteem, diminish your energy to accomplish life tasks, and generally aren't even true. If someone asks, "What are you not good at doing?" you might say, "I'm not mechanical," or "I'm not good at math," or "I'm not good at writing," or "I'm not much of a people person." Not only do these labels damage your self-esteem, they are usually based on one negative experience in which you either struggled with a related task or received critical feedback that you took to heart. Another harmful impact of labels is that you may find yourself expending a great deal of energy avoiding any activity that even hints at what you've been labeled as lacking. The consequences can range from minor to major, especially if you're avoiding many activities and situations.

Many of those old limiting beliefs and labels come from childhood experiences and may or may not have been accurate assessments of you as a child and may be even less accurate assessments of you in the present. Retest as many of these old labels as is reasonably possible, rather than merely accepting them as true. For example, if you have basic math or public speaking anxieties, enroll in a class that teaches relaxation techniques along with the basic skills. Or try taking a noncredit, adult education course in which you can learn skills without the pressure of being graded.

Sometimes a family system labels you "not something" simply because someone else in the family "is something." And comparatively, you may not seem to do well at that skill because the family members have such a high standard for it that they fail to acknowledge that anything less than excelling is legitimate. Or a family may believe that only one person in the family can be good at a specific skill. If an older sibling or a parent has "claimed" that skill no other family member is allowed to demonstrate it.

Although you may not be the best in your family at a certain skill or you may lack a natural ability for a particular skill, you're not absolutely lacking in that skill. You might ask yourself what might have made it difficult for your family to acknowledge or support your development and expression of certain skills. How did the limiting labels you received reflect family beliefs and values about what was acceptable versus unacceptable, what was valued versus devalued, or what was appropriate versus inappropriate for males versus females? What new messages can you give yourself about those labels?

Many times we base assumptions on those old limiting labels, whether they came from our family or society, and it's important to challenge them. Perhaps you're not naturally talented at mechanical skills, but I challenge you to find a three-year-old who can change the oil in a car. All skills are learned. Some people have natural abilities in certain areas and learn those skills easier and to a greater depth than other people, but that does not mean those skills are out of reach for you. Don't confuse being gifted in a certain skill with being able to develop competence in that skill given effort and time.

SKILLS AS A MATTER OF DEGREE

Possessing skills is not an all-or-nothing condition. You either have milk in your refrigerator or you don't, but it is not true that you absolutely are 100% competent in a skill or you don't possess it at all. You don't even have to be in the top 10% of all people who have a skill to possess that skill. You may trudge your way through a math class or drag yourself through a writing assignment or a committee meeting and feel awkward and out of place. You are not, however, without skill in that area; it may just not be a skill strength for you.

You have skills and you have skill strengths. When you interview for a job, you want to stress your skill strengths—the things that you do really well, that you have mastered. You can possess the essence of a skill without mastering it. Don't say, "Yeah, I can type 40 wpm, but I don't feel like I can really type because I should be able to type 80 wpm." If you can type 40 wpm, you can type; it's still a skill that you possess. It may not be developed to the level you want, but it's still your skill.

Some of us need to be in the top 10% of all people who have that skill, for example, neurosurgeons. I don't want someone operating on my brain who has only a so-so grasp of that skill. In other jobs your tasks are not life-threatening and you can develop skill and deepen your knowledge and ability over time without any irreversible or detrimental impact to anyone.

Assess your ability level on the skill that you want to develop. Where are you now, and where would you like to be or need to be? This is also not an all or nothing situation. It's not as though you need to learn each skill you want to develop from ground zero, although that might occasionally be the case. Usually, you will have some baseline skill ability in an area; for example, you may need to speed up your typing or learn one more computer program. Avoid global, inaccurate assessments, such as "I need to learn how to write." A more accurate assessment may be that you need to learn how to develop stronger conclusions in your business reports. This goal is specific, more manageable, and more measurable.

In addition, consider which skills you need to learn now and which you can learn later, and prioritize them in order of importance. Create a list of career-based skill development goals for yourself and divide it into two columns: Skills I Want to Build on and Skills I Want to Learn. Depending on the careers or jobs that you decide to pursue, you can decide which skills to learn now and which you can learn later.

It's also useful to ask others which skills they think you need to develop to be attractive to a prospective employer in a particular job setting. One good way to do this is through an *informational interview:* You contact individuals working in the jobs you're considering, and ask them which skills they use daily on the job. Often, the skills you acquire in a training program will not perfectly match the skills you'll need on the job.

Career centers offer various informational interview formats that you can draw from in creating your interview questions. Basic questions include these topics: the training needed, skills used on the job, the most- and least-appealing aspects of the job, prospects for advancement, salary and benefits, future trends in the field, and advice about how you should proceed.

One good reason for doing an informational interview, even if you're just entering a training program, is that you may develop skills in a training program that you use very little on the job, and you may need on-the-job skills that aren't taught in the training program. It's also useful to know the percentage of time you actually use a skill on the job. For example, in a training program you get the sense that person-to-person interaction will occur 15 percent of the time, but you find out that on the job it's actually 30 percent of the time if you include face-to-face and phone contact. Knowing this in advance can help you gauge whether the job is a good match for you in terms of who you are, your values, and your skill development.

You may have the option of learning skills on the job, rather than in some kind of official training program. Many companies hire people who have baseline skills that can be developed and fine-tuned to meet the exact needs of a specific job. This option may better suit your individual circumstances, preferences, and needs in terms of learning new skills.

Focus on Skills

Looking Within

Write as many endings to each sentence as you can.

1. What I have learned to do (in school, at work, or in other life situations)...

2. I get great enjoyment from...

3. Things that come easily for me...

Sneak Preview of Your Informational Interview

This exercise section is designed to help you create a list of questions that you can use to gather the career information most pertinent to your preferences and personality. Below are several prepared questions, along with space for you to write any additional questions that you may have. Read through the questions and transfer those most applicable to you to the informational interview compilation list at the end of Chapter 9. Feel free to practice asking students, family, and friends these questions to help you ascertain what is most important to you.

1. What skills are required for this job?
2. Which skills can I learn on the job?
3. Which skills are used the most day to day?
4. Which skills are most valued?
5. Which skills lead to career advancement?

Add your personalized questions here:

6.

7.

8.

4. Things I learned at an early age...

Note: You may find that some skills appear more than once or that no skills overlap for each question—either is absolutely fine.

Sorting Your Skills

Part I

Step 1: Turn back to the two skill lists you constructed at the beginning of the chapter. Write each skill on a separate 3" × 5" index card. On the back of each card write what you like about the skill. If you like absolutely nothing about it, write what you dislike about it.

Step 2: Turn the cards back over to their fronts. Sort them into three piles: Like, Dislike, and Willing to Do.

Step 3: Sort the Like pile into two piles: Current Skills and Unlearned Skills. These Like piles correspond to the "very good fit" inner section of the skills wedge on your On Target model. Write those skills here. You will use this information later in the Wedge Work exercise at the end of this chapter.

Step 4: Sort the Willing to Do pile into two piles: Current Skills and Unlearned Skills. These Willing to Do piles correspond to the "adequate fit" middle section of the skills wedge on your On Target model. Write those skills here. You will use this information later in the Wedge Work exercise at the end of this chapter.

Step 5: Sort the Dislike pile into two piles: Current Skills and Unlearned Skills. These Dislike piles correspond to the "unacceptable fit" outer section of the skills wedge on your On Target model. Write those skills here. You will use this information later in the Wedge Work exercise at the end of this chapter.

Part II

Step 1: Place your skill cards in one stack. Read each one and place it in one of two piles: Pile 1 is any skill that comes easily, that you learned early in life or do well currently; Pile 2 is any skill you have not yet learned or struggle with, or for which you are still developing basic abilities.

Step 2: Look again at the cards in Pile 1—these are your current skill strengths that you can use and stress when appropriate and applicable on resumés, job interviews, and cover letters. Once the skills in Pile 2 are developed and improved, you can add them to your other skill strengths in Pile 1. For now, think about how you could gain or improve the skills in Pile 2. Jot down your ideas here:

Part III

Place your skill cards in one stack, with the side stating what you like or dislike facing up. See if you can sort these likes and dislikes into common categories—any kinds of categories are acceptable. Look for key words as clues to categories: working with people, creating beautiful things, having personal freedom, having a sense of accomplishment, getting to see a finished product, feeling comfortable or competent doing the skill, helping others, liking the challenge of problem-solving, and so on.

You may find that some cards don't fit into any obvious grouping; that's fine, just leave them separate. You can use this information to look for themes in your categories and then use those themes as clues to what to look for in career possibilities to enhance your feelings of job satisfaction. You can develop a checklist of your categories as a step to exploring job possibilities and making certain that key components are present. Also, these categories connect directly to what you value and find meaningful, and whenever a job choice can encompass key values and personal meaning, the more comfortably the job will fit other aspects of yourself.

Microskills Activity

Microskills is a combination of a paper and pencil exercise and a computer-sorting process. Career centers at community colleges and universities have Microskills. The Microskills worksheet lists over 70 skills. Select 35 skills in order of preference that you would most enjoy using in a future career. The computer matches these skills to the skills used in various occupations and the computer produces a list of 30 occupations that most closely incorporate the skills you indicated you wanted to use on the job.

What I like most about Microskills is that it focuses on the skills you would like to use in a career, not merely on the skills you currently have. This is especially important for someone who has taken ability-based skill tests that indicate that she should continue in a job that she wants to or needs to leave. Instead, Microskills focuses on the skills you would feel positive about using in a career.

Exploring Career Options

Consult the computer printout of careers generated by Microskills. Choose 10 careers from this list that you find potentially appealing and are willing to consider as possible options:

1.

2.

3.

4.

5.

6.

7.

8.

9.

10.

Now highlight the five most appealing careers to explore and gather information on. Go to your school, library, or career center and investigate these careers.

Once you've explored these careers, you may find that your top five career options have changed. Did you discover related careers that looked appealing? Based on the research you've done, what are your top five career options now?

Write your updated career list here:

1.

2.

3.

4.

5.

Exploring Skills Associated with Careers

Based on your career options research, what's your best guess of the skills used and valued in your top five career options? In the following chart, list each career option. Beside each option, list each skill in the column that best describes how you feel about using that skill. You can determine the accuracy of your skill list once you've done the informational interviews.

	Skills		
Career Option	Very Good Fit	Adequate Fit	Unacceptable Fit
1.			
2.			
3.			
4.			
5.			

Wedge Work

Figure 4.1 shows an On Target model with the Skills wedge containing some sample skills. You can use these samples to get an idea of how filling in these wedges works. Earlier in this chapter, you made a list of skills, some things that you do well, and a list of skills you want to develop. Now, drawing from both those lists, you want to place these skills in either the blank Survival Skills wedge, as shown in Figure 4.2, or the Growth Skills wedge, as shown in Figure 4.3. To remind yourself of the distinctions between Growth and Survival modes, see Chapter 1.

In the Very Good Fit innermost section of each wedge, list the words that represent skills you consider essential to use in your work. In the Adequate Fit middle section, list words that reflect skills you'd like to use in your work, those that would enhance the quality of your life but that aren't essential. In the Unacceptable Fit outer section, jot down those skills that you would not want present in your work, those that would make doing your work nearly impossible.

Once you have a sense that you have gathered all of the essential information about yourself onto the enlarged skill wedge, you can then transfer it to your growth and survival copies of the On Target model in Chapter 8.

Consider These Questions...

1. What have you learned about your skill strengths?

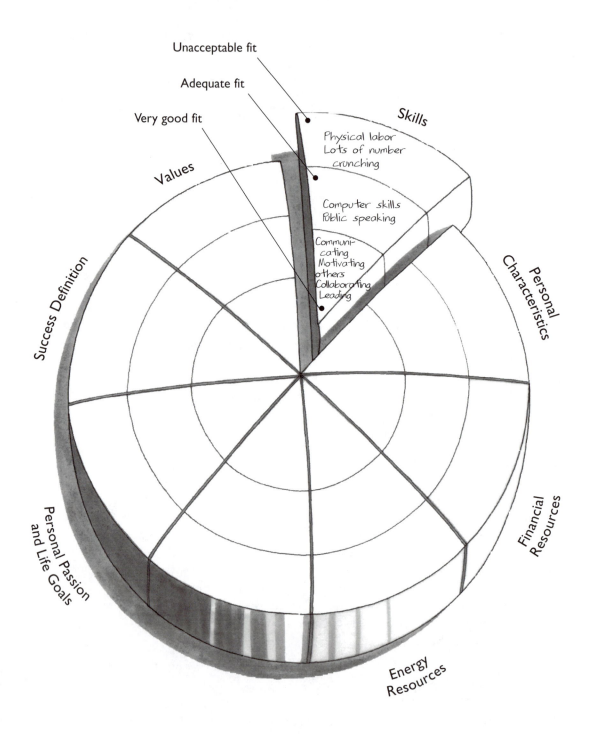

FIGURE 4.1   An On Target model, with the *Skills* wedge filled in with sample skills.

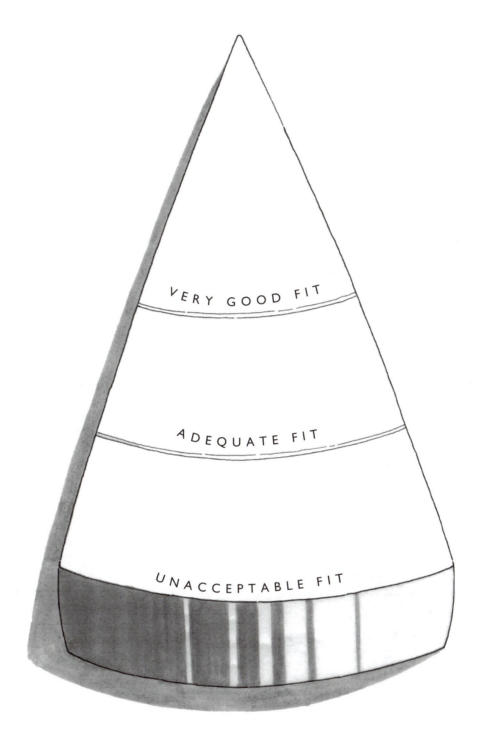

FIGURE 4.2   A blank *Survival Skills* wedge, ready for you to add words that describe your skills.

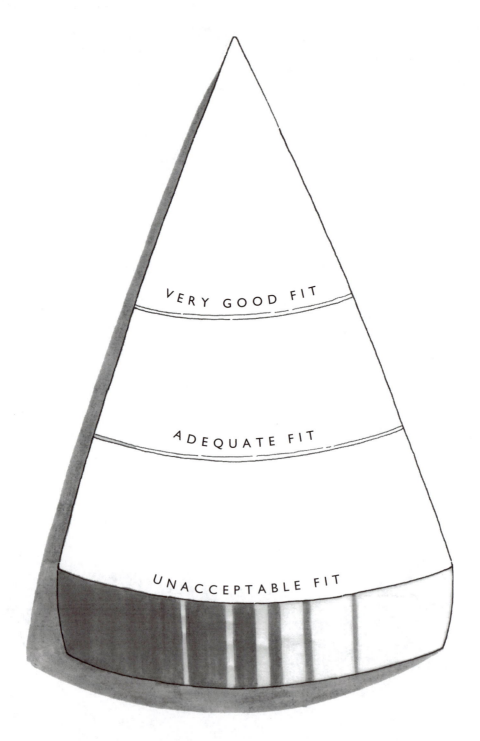

FIGURE 4.3 A blank *Growth Skills* wedge, ready for you to add words that describe skills you would like to develop, or current skills you would like to use.

2. What did you find most appealing or interesting regarding your top five careers?

3. What additional questions do you have about those five careers?

Ideas for Action

Use this space to write down thoughts, leads, ideas, and questions that you want to pursue.

Things to explore now   *Things to explore later*

RECOMMENDED READING

Bolton, Robert. *People Skills*. New York: Simon and Schuster, 1986.
Presents a thorough approach to improving personal performance and communications skills.

McKay, Matthew, Martha Davis, and Patrick Fanning. *Messages: The Communication Skills Book*. Oakland: New Harbinger Publications, 1993.
Provides assistance in developing essential communication skills and increasing interpersonal effectiveness.

Sher, Barbara. *Wishcraft*. New York: Ballantine, 1979.
Helps in uncovering skills and abilities, in developing a support network for achieving goals and dreams, and in formulating techniques for continued motivation.

5

MIRROR, MIRROR
·······························
Personal Characteristics and Identity Issues

SEEING YOURSELF CLEARLY

Seeing yourself clearly is seeing the best and the worst aspects of yourself with equal clarity. It is identifying, at least to yourself, your best characteristics as well as your struggles, challenges, and weaknesses. When you see yourself clearly, you do not necessarily accept, like, or enjoy all aspects; but, in the privacy of your own thoughts, you can say, "This is who I truly am, not who I represent to the world, not who others see, not who I attempt to appear, but who I truly am."

Seeing yourself clearly is difficult. Most of us go back and forth between overperceiving and overemphasizing our limitations and failings and overestimating and overfocusing on our strengths. We swing from devaluing ourselves and seeing ourselves as nothing more than our limitations and failings to overvaluing our strengths and not being realistic about our genuine limitations.

Realistically assessing your strengths and limitations gives you important information. And as you saw in Chapter 4, when you see your skills clearly, you can make decisions about what skills you need to develop, either personally or professionally. When you see your strengths clearly, you know what you have to offer an employer, or what you have to offer if you're opening your own business.

Another piece of the overperceiving or underperceiving dilemma involves the "I'm not good at anything" and "I could do anything if I tried" statements. Again, most people vacillate between the two, and, like most things, the truth lies somewhere in the middle. Some days you feel as if you can't do anything right, and that everyone is mad at you. On other days when you shine, you feel exuberant, and everything seems possible. In reality, most of us are not constructed entirely of our limitations or entirely of limitless possibilities—most of us are a blending.

Most of us also have many "selves," which can be compared to concentric rings. In the center are the selves only we know and perhaps some selves we don't know—those outside our conscious awareness. The rings closest to the center contain the selves that our family and very close friends know. The rings on the outermost edges of the circle contain those selves that a grocery cashier or a postal carrier might know.

Everyone knows a slightly different aspect of you. If you worked in a job that required you to be extroverted and your true self is introverted, coworkers may consider you very outgoing because your job necessitated that kind of behavior. The same coworkers might be surprised to find you quite inward and introverted at a social function.

Our exterior self often is not congruent with our interior self. That duality is the result of playing multiple roles in the world. In the midst of playing out these many roles, however, each individual needs a clear sense of who he truly is in his inner world. Even if a particular job or career does not allow an outward expression, each person must retain a true inner sense of identity.

You might be asking, What's the point in even bothering to know myself clearly when what I really need is a new job? Seeing yourself clearly has several benefits. One is it becomes easier to make decisions about which skills to develop, how best to use your strengths, and how to reduce or eliminate your limitations and information gaps.

Also, the closer we are to our true selves, the more we can safely and accurately share those selves with others and the less complicated and stressful our lives become. This occurs because we're not having to continually demonstrate who we are or clear up misconceptions based on our outer expressions or behaviors that don't match how we feel inside.

Having a congruent, accurate, in-line sense of who you are, of how you feel about things, of your reactions, and of what is important to you saves a lot of time. You might also want to compare how you view yourself with how others view you. How much alignment is there between the views of people who know you relatively well and your view of yourself?

Below is a list of personal characteristics. Circle those that best describe how you currently see yourself. Add any characteristics that describe you that aren't on the list. Place a checkmark by any characteristic that you would like to express in a work setting. Place a double checkmark by any characteristic that you want to be certain to avoid in a work setting. You will use this information later in the Wedge Work section at the end of this chapter. You might also want to ask others to read through a photocopy of this list and circle the characteristics they feel best describe you. This information can provide useful insights into how you are perceived and may uncover characteristics of which you were not aware. Choose only people you trust, and take their feedback simply as additional input rather than as a definitive statement or evaluation of you.

Personal Characteristics List

accurate	enterprising	powerful
active	enthusiastic	private
adaptable	excited	purposeful
agile	factual	questioning
agreeable	fair	quiet
alert	faithful	realistic
approachable	generous	reasonable
brave	genuine	reliable
bright	helpful	respectful
busy	humorous	responsible
capable	impactful	restrained
careful	independent	risk-taking
caring	intelligent	satisfied
clear	intense	self-sufficient
clever	involved	sensitive
committed	joyful	sincere
compassionate	kind	stable
compliant	leading	strict
conforming	lively	strong
creative	loving	sympathetic
courageous	loyal	tactful
daring	meticulous	tenacious
dependable	modest	thorough
determined	neat	trustworthy
dexterous	nonconformist	truthful
directing	objective	understanding
eager	orderly	versatile
efficient	patient	wise
energetic	peaceful	witty
engaged	persistent	worldly

BEING WHO YOU WANT TO BE, NOT WHO OTHERS WANT YOU TO BE

It takes real courage to continue or to start being who you want to be rather than who others want you to be. Other people are often highly invested in ensuring that you continue to be the way they have always perceived you. Growth and change in you and in your behavior can be very threatening and unsettling to other people. On the other hand, if you continue to be who you are and that doesn't match the preferences of others, they can in subtle or obvious ways continually pressure you to match their preferences.

It also takes courage to risk others' disapproval, to endure distancing behaviors when they don't care for how you are behaving, and to risk losing their emotional and financial support. Some people can be highly punitive and/or reactive when you start trying to follow your true self. Most of us have a real need to feel that the people and things around us have continuity and that they won't change in the future. Someone who's known you for years and feels that she can usually predict your behavior can be very confused to find that suddenly what and who she thought you were is not really who you are now. Without meaning to impede your growth process, there can be everything from rampant questions such as "Why are you acting like that?" or "Why are you doing that?" or "How come you're saying those things?" to downright punitive responses such as, "I don't want to be with you if you're going to be like that," or "Well, if that's what you're thinking about for a career, I'm not going to help you out with tuition or day care or moving if you need to relocate."

Most people, when reacting in a negative way to your changes, are responding out of fear, not out of intentions to see you hurt or unable to keep growing. They fear that if you grow and change and become who you really want to be, they'll lose you, or their connection with you. One thing that can be very helpful is to sit down with the important people in your life, inform them about your change process, and talk together about its impact on them. Often, you can ease people's fears by assuring them that your relationships will continue and that you'd like support and encouragement for this new emerging part of yourself.

Another way you can ease people's fears, and perhaps your own, is to take an attitude of experimentation toward exploring who you want to be. I encourage people to view all potential personal qualities as neither positive nor negative. Instead, how the quality is used determines its positive or negative value. For example, a person who is too persistent doesn't know when to walk away from an unrewarding or damaging situation. A person who is not persistent enough does not know how to encounter challenging circumstances without giving up. Persistence itself is neither positive nor negative; how it's used in a situation determines whether it's positive or negative.

A thermostat is a good analogy. Too little heat is painful, and too much heat is miserable. Heat though, is neither positive nor negative unless it matches or does not match the needs of the situation. A comfort zone is established when it matches. You can apply this "comfort zone" thermostat approach to any personal quality or characteristic that you're working to develop or that you're expressing to more fully be who you want to be.

Let's say you want to be more assertive in your interactions with others. Rather than, "I can't ever seem to be assertive," say, "My assertiveness thermostat seems to be turned down low. How can I best adjust it into a comfort zone?" You then gradually raise your assertiveness setting by slowly engaging in bits of assertive behavior when possible. The helpful aspect of the thermostat analogy is that it can help you stay out of the mind-set that you either absolutely have or fail to have a certain characteristic. No one is totally without assertiveness or any other quality—it's a matter of adjusting the level of that quality so that it matches your picture of how you want to be.

Personal characteristics that I'd like to raise my thermostat setting on:

1.   6.
2.   7.
3.   8.
4.   9.
5.   10.

Personal characteristics that I'd like to lower my thermostat setting on:

1.   6.
2.   7.
3.   8.
4.   9.
5.   10.

Personal characteristics that are currently in my comfort zone:

1.   6.
2.   7.
3.   8.
4.   9.
5.   10.

Some characteristics may respond to self-initiated change, and others may indicate deep personality aspects and be less responsive to initial change attempts. A rule of thumb is to work at adjusting the expression of a given personal characteristic. If using your best change strategies and those of others cannot effect the change, seek outside assistance. If you have any questions regarding personality assessment, seek a licensed mental health professional who is trained to administer an inventory and interpret the information.

BEING WHO YOU WANT TO BECOME

Don't wait for good self-esteem to show up to do what you want in your life. So many people feel that if they only felt better about themselves and that if they only had more confidence, more belief in themselves, and more support from other people, they could start accomplishing what they want to do and be who they want to be. They keep waiting for the sense of self-esteem to kick in, which will give them the go-ahead to say, "Okay, I'm all together, I can do these things."

Self-esteem comes out of action and out of attempts or trying; it doesn't emerge as the result of accomplishments or achievements or from what we might think of as successes. For example, a child builds a sense of competence by attempting to walk across the room without falling down. The child may fall down dozens of times, but each attempt builds on the previous attempts and gradually builds competence.

It's the same way with self-esteem. If you start moving forward as though you deserve what you're pursuing, as though you can trust your judgment, as though it's important for you to do that, most of the time the feelings will follow. You act as if you already possess what you are striving to obtain.

Let's say you want to feel more confident, more self-reliant, or more purposeful. Rather than wait for those feelings to come, act as if you have them. Ask yourself, "What would a confident person do in this situation?" and do your best to emulate that behavior. When you engage in self-reliant behavior, self-reliant feelings often emerge. If you sit and wait for the feelings to appear before you take on that characteristic or that quality, you can be waiting a very long time.

Another approach is to be as many pieces of what you want to become as you possibly can be and not get hung up on waiting until all the pieces are in place before you own that quality. Perhaps your issue is self-confidence. You can feel self-confident in certain settings and around certain people or if you're well-rested or if the discussion concerns certain topics. Own that self-confidence now. Don't say, "Well, I have to wait until I feel globally self-confident in every situation before I can really be and consider myself a self-confident person." Own it now, even if only little tidbits are showing up. Walk around as if that's the full truth of you, and you'll gradually grow into it.

You can be intellectually aware that it's not the full truth of you in all circumstances or on all days; nonetheless, it's the process of being who you want to become, and it's an ongoing process. You're not a batch of muffins that, when fully done, can come out of the oven and that's it. You're constantly evolving and changing. Who you decide you want to become, at some point, becomes who you are now, and who you then want to become will be something entirely different. That's part of the wonder, magic, and excitement of life; so give yourself permission to be what you're beginning to grow to be right now.

Focus on Personal Characteristics

Looking Within

Write as many endings to each sentence as you can.

1. My current strengths...

2. My current limitations...

3. The best thing about my true self...

4. The hardest thing about others' disapproval...

Exploring Personal Characteristics Associated with Careers

Based on your career options research, what's your best guess of the personal characteristics needed or allowed expression in your top five career options? List each career option. The list of personal characteristics provided earlier in this chapter may help you. You can determine the accuracy of your personal characteristics list once you've done the informational interviews. (See Chapter 4 for details on informational interviews.)

Sneak Preview of Your Informational Interview

This exercise section is designed to help you create a list of questions that you can use to gather the career information most pertinent to your preferences and personality. Below are several prepared questions, along with space for you to write additional questions. Read through the questions and transfer those most applicable to you to the informational interview compilation list at the end of Chapter 9. Feel free to practice asking students, family, and friends these questions to help you ascertain what is most important.

1. What personal characteristics do you need to do this job well?
2. Of these characteristics, which two are the most important for this job?
3. What personal characteristics don't fit or would make it difficult to do this job?
4. These personal characteristics (list them) are my strengths. How do they fit with this job?
5. How would these characteristics be used on the job?

Include your additional personalized questions here:

6.

7.

8.

Career Option	Personal Characteristics		
	Very Good Fit	Adequate Fit	Unacceptable Fit
1.			
2.			
3.			
4.			
5.			

Wedge Work

Figure 5.1 shows an On Target model with the Personal Characteristics wedge containing some sample personal characteristics. You can use these samples to get an idea of how filling in these wedges works. Earlier in this chapter, you made a list of your own personal characteristics. Now you want to place these in either the blank Survival Personal Characteristics wedge, as shown in Figure 5.2, or the Growth Personal Characteristics wedge, as shown in Figure 5.3. To remind yourself of the distinctions between Growth and Survival modes, see Chapter 1.

In the Very Good Fit innermost section of each wedge, list the words that represent the personal characteristics you consider essential to express in your work. In the Adequate Fit middle section, list words that reflect personal characteristics you'd like to express in your work, those that would enhance the quality of your life but that aren't essential. In the Unacceptable Fit outer section, jot down those personal characteristics that you would not want to express in your work, those that would make doing your work nearly impossible.

Once you have a sense that you have gathered all of the essential information about yourself onto the enlarged personal characteristics wedge, transfer that information to your growth and survival copies of the On Target model in Chapter 8.

Consider These Questions…

1. What have you learned about your personal characteristics?

2. How do you respond or cope with others' disapproval regarding these characteristics?

3. What characteristics would you like to act as if you already possess and what might help you to do that?

VERY GOOD FIT

ADEQUATE FIT

UNACCEPTABLE FIT

FIGURE 5.3 A blank *Growth Personal Characteristics* wedge, ready for you to add words that describe personal characteristics you would like to develop or current personal characteristics you would like to use.

Ideas for Action

Use this space to write down thoughts, leads, ideas, and questions that you want to pursue.

Things to explore now   *Things to explore later*

RECOMMENDED READING

Hirsh, Sandra, and Jean Kummerow. *Life Types*. Palo Alto: Time Warner, 1989.

Helps in understanding personality style by using exercises based on the Myers-Briggs Type Indicator. Provides you with a psychological self-portrait.

Matthews, Andrew. *Being Happy!* Los Angeles: Price Stern Sloan, 1990.

A light-hearted, easy-to-read book that focuses on increasing self-awareness, self-confidence, and goal achievement.

Minchinton, Jerry. *Maximum Self-Esteem*. Vanzant, MI: Arnford House, 1993.

Focuses on reducing the causes, rather than just the symptoms, of low self-esteem by learning to shed false beliefs and ceasing to dislike yourself.

6

"GO" POWER

Discovering and Using Your Resources

When we talk about resources in the context of the On Target model, we're looking at finances and energy—aspects of your situation and yourself that you can draw on to make your life work, to help move you through and fuel your career-change process so that you can reach your goals.

IDENTIFYING RESOURCES

Financial resources are those that you'll need to support yourself while changing careers, especially if a component of your plan is retraining or an educational degree. Also, financial resources include those that you'll need in your next job or career so that you can adequately support your life style.

Make a list of any financial resources you have or would like to develop:

Resources you have

1.

2.

3.

4.

5.

6.

7.

8.

9.

10.

Resources you want to develop

1.

2.

3.

4.

5.

6.

7.

8.

9.

10.

Energy resources are those that determine how much emotion, time, and physical activity you can devote to a career change. Are you a parent with three children under the age of 10? If so, your energy resources will be different from those of someone with three children who have graduated from high school or from those of someone without children. Do you have physical challenges that affect your energy levels? These and other such factors affect how much energy you have to expend in a career-change process—in retraining, in education, or in a job search.

Now, consider your emotional resources. How much emotional energy do you have at this point in your life?

Which emotional resources would you like to develop?

How many of your emotional resources are currently going toward other people and how many are free to expend in learning a new job? Emotional resources can also include strong personal characteristics that you identified in Chapter 5. Remember, resources are any aspects of your situation or yourself that you can draw on to make your life work.

Your energy resources also have an impact on how much energy you can expend daily on the job. Your other life responsibilities and priorities, combined with your current energy level, dictate the amount of energy you can direct toward your work. One individual may find a 60-hour work week that involves lots of traveling appealing; another person may find that job not even remotely possible or appealing.

In addition, look at your time resources. How much time can you comfortably devote to the career-change process?

How much time are you be willing to devote to your work on a daily, ongoing basis?

It's helpful to be realistic about your resources, both in terms of what you have to expend and what you're willing to expend. If you are realistic, you can be much clearer in your decision making. You can also avoid setting yourself up for a situation that will overextend you and your resources or be a poor fit for you at this point in your life.

The good news is that as we change and grow, so do our resources and our willingness to use them in different arenas in our lives. You aren't making a final decision about how you will always allocate your resources; you're just being realistic about what those resources are now and how you will expend them.

It's also helpful to identify resources that are constants in your life. Constant resources are those that are reasonably consistent and are a solid part of you regardless of what else is occurring in your life. One of my constant resources is that I can comfortably get by on six hours of sleep no matter what's going on in my life. Thus, I have a somewhat greater time resource than someone who needs ten hours to function well.

There are also situational resources that you can access in some circumstances. It's summertime and Shelley isn't coaching high school sports. For the duration of the summer, Shelley can access extra energy that isn't available to her during the school year.

Another important step is to identify resources that you have had or used in the past, that you currently don't have, but that you might be able to access in the future. For example, you used to be very efficient and organized and accomplished a lot in a day. Because of what's transpired for you in the past few years, you no longer access that resource, but you know it's still a part of you, even if it's in hibernation. When we look at building and developing resources later in this chapter, you may decide to take those resources out of hibernation. For now, simply write them down.

KNOWING YOURSELF: STRENGTHS, GAPS, LIMITATIONS, AND OTHER CONCERNS

In this section, we'll look at how you can be clear and honest with yourself about your strengths, gaps, and limitations. Also, we'll look at any special considerations or concerns that could affect your recareering process. In the On Target model, one of the eight wedges is left untitled so that you can indicate any special considerations that might limit or shape the fit between your personal concerns or needs and possible career choices.

Acknowledging your limitations is very different from being self-critical and disliking yourself, saying, "I don't have this and I haven't developed that yet, and I'm less valuable or worthwhile because of it." Identifying your strengths and limitations is about clearly assessing what you have going for you, where your gaps are, and where you haven't had the chance to build resources. This clear-eyed assessment will provide valuable information you can use to make well-considered decisions. The good news is that most resources, like skills, can be developed, learned, or enhanced to help you create what you want in life.

In the first section of this chapter, you did your best to identify some of your current resources. Go back to those lists and put a check by the resources that you feel are significant strengths—those you can rely on, that have the potential to move you toward your goal.

Which items on your list of resources might serve as limitations?

Are those items in the time category, in the finances category, or in some other category? How might you be limited by those resources?

How might this affect your career-change process or choices?

Focusing on your limitations and gaps is an act of self-awareness, self-knowing, and self-esteem. I believe people exhibit a lack of self-esteem when they need to convince themselves or others that they have no limitations. Having limitations just means that there is an edge, a boundary, or a fence around what's possible for you. It doesn't mean you can't pick up the fence post, scoot the fence out, and give yourself a larger expanse of what's possible. Acknowledging limitations is simply a way of saying that certain things may not be possible for you right now. Not only is this perfectly appropriate, it's also a crucial part of balancing what you feel passionate about and what's possible.

It's also important to identify gaps in your resources. Which resources haven't you fully developed?

Which resources do you need to add or further develop?

We'll focus on this in the next section of this chapter.

It's also essential to trust your perceptions about your strengths, gaps, and limitations. You may find yourself looking at these questions and feeling uncertain, thinking, "I believe these are my strengths, but I'm not sure" or "I could be limited by these things, but maybe I'm just needlessly worrying" or "I'm not seeing any gaps, I don't know what's wrong."

If this is the case, talk with someone whose judgment you trust, whose insight and ability to view objectively who you are is reliable. Use this person as a sounding board, first of all to talk out these questions and issues. Second, see if you can get additional clarity. If you still feel stuck, ask why this person perceives you or your resources in certain ways.

Now let's look at special considerations and concerns. We've talked about a handful of different kinds of resources—financial, emotional, and time. In addition, it's important to look at other considerations that might shape what you're able to do or choose in your career-change process. For example, do you have disabilities or any physical limitations that need special consideration? How might your choices affect an important relationship or relationships? Adults who are primary caregivers for aging parents need to make life choices around the declining health of an older parent.

A back injury could be a physical limitation. A learning disability might be a limitation. If you find reading and retaining information difficult, you might need to shape a job choice around that. Recovery issues—substance abuse, physical abuse, or sexual abuse—can be limiting. Certain work environments aren't conducive or supportive to recovery issues. You might need special considerations for parenting or for your spiritual practices—whatever feels important to you that is not addressed in the other seven wedges of the On Target model. Place those concerns in the untitled wedge.

BUILDING AND DEVELOPING NEW RESOURCES

Return to your initial list. Did you identify resources that you'd like to build on or develop? Brainstorm with others about possible resource options. What resources do they draw on? If someone has been able to develop or create resources that appeal to you but that you haven't been able to acquire, ask how he did it. Would he help you? Would he be your mentor?

Two useful ways to increase your resources are developing financial management and time management skills.

Financial Management Skills

Financial management skills are essential; your financial needs and resources influence your career options. One good way to start is to track all your income and expenses for an entire month. Do your expenses exceed your income or does your income meet or exceed your expenses? If your income does not meet your expenses, you can either increase the money you earn or decrease the money you spend. Most cities have consumer credit counselors who are happy to help you devise a reasonable budget that accommodates your needs and decreases your expenses.

Budgets are really nothing more than a To Do list for your money. By identifying how you spend your money each month, you can create a budget that includes ongoing expenses—food, transportation, housing, and so on—and intermittent expenses, such as tuition and travel. Most people find that they benefit from creating both a monthly budget and a long-range financial plan. A long-range financial plan allows you to set major financial goals and to identify the steps to achieve them. Whether your goals are to purchase a house, attend college, or invest, a long-range financial plan allows you to determine the financial steps you need to take each month to make your goals a reality. You can then incorporate those financial steps into your monthly budget and create a timeline of x number of months that it will take to achieve your goals.

In addition, if attending college is a component in your career-change process, you need a clear picture of your finances as well as information regarding funding and financial assistance. Nearly all community colleges and universities have a financial aid office that can give you information about loans, grants, work-study programs, scholarships, and additional sources of funding for higher education.

Time Management Skills

Time management is crucial to your overall sense of well-being as well as to your ability to make the most of your other resources and opportunities. Without some form of time management in your life, you will be more likely to use your financial, emotional, and physical resources less effectively. Each of us has 168 hours each week, and we all vary in how well we utilize that time. If your use of time works well for you, continue sustaining your current abilities in this area and focus your energy on strengthening other resources.

If your use of time isn't serving you well, here are some suggestions to help you start making better use of your time. View a schedule as a time budget in which you make decisions in advance about how you will spend your limited resources. In the same manner as you did for your finances, keep a record of how you spend your time, focusing on what you do and how long you do it. Instead of recording this information for a month, however, track it for one week.

On the following pages is a scheduling sheet that lists the days of the week and the hours of the day in 30-minute intervals from 6:00 A.M. until midnight. Feel free to make your own chart expanding or adjusting the hours to reflect your needs. You may be wondering why the schedule is broken into 30-minute slots. Most tasks rarely need exact intervals of an hour or multiples of an hour to be completed. Every time you round an activity to the next hour, you round off time that you could use elsewhere. By making purposeful use of those time segments, you can accumulate extra hours of productive time each week.

Start filling in the schedule by listing all the recurring activities first, such as work, school, sleeping, eating, commuting, and so on. Now schedule other responsibilities that are more flexible, such as studying, exercising, socializing, and running errands. Don't forget to add travel time between activities if necessary.

Look at how you spent your time during the week. Were you able to complete your tasks? Did you squander much time—time in which you neither accomplished a task nor allowed yourself to fully relax? Was much time eaten up by unexpected delays? Were you caught waiting and unable to use that time? One way to counteract that dilemma is to always carry small tasks with you—reading material, paperwork, and correspondence, for example.

Utilizing your responses to the above questions as well as a simple scheduling method, you can begin to create a schedule that works well for you. It is also helpful to revise or adapt your schedule before the start of each new week, to adjust to your needs, obligations, and priorities. Refer to the record you kept, and make certain that the schedule you're currently filling in reflects your needs that emerged. Don't forget to schedule time for fun, and build in small free time breaks. If your schedule is extremely crowded for a given week, you can gain additional time by whittling down the amount of time a task usually takes and applying that extra time to another task. Or you can move tasks that don't need immediate attention to your next week's schedule or delegate some tasks to other individuals. By taking the time to create a realistic time management schedule, you create more control in your life by using the resources you possess more wisely. In addition, by using your time more wisely, you create the opportunity to uncover and explore other resources that you may need to help you achieve your goals.

EXTERNAL AND INTERNAL RESOURCES

You can identify the resources that you need by determining which are internal and which are external. Examples of internal resources are determination, commitment, desire, or coping skills and usually can only be altered by your working on aspects of yourself. Examples of external resources are finances, commuting time, or additional help with child care and often can be altered by you and others. When people in your life express a desire to assist in your career-change process, they can usually do so with external resources. You can also request that they contribute by encouraging and supporting you in developing your internal resources.

In addition, determine whether your resource gaps are survival-based or growth-based. You usually need to develop survival resources before developing growth resources. In other words, financial resources and maintaining important relationships will take precedence over having more time to go on vacation or garden. Some people might say, however, that if they don't garden, they don't feel they're surviving. The distinction between survival resources and growth resources is an individual matter.

	Sun.	Mon.	Tues.	Wed.	Thur.	Fri.	Sat.
6:00							
6:30							
7:00							
7:30							
8:00							
8:30							
9:00							
9:30							
10:00							
10:30							
11:00							
11:30							
12:00							
12:30							
1:00							
1:30							
2:00							
2:30							

	Sun.	Mon.	Tues.	Wed.	Thur.	Fri.	Sat.
3:00							
3:30							
4:00							
4:30							
5:00							
5:30							
6:00							
6:30							
7:00							
7:30							
8:00							
8:30							
9:00							
9:30							
10:00							
10:30							
11:00							
11:30							
12:00							

It's also a good idea to determine which resources you want to build or develop next and which can wait. You might find that you've put a lot of time into maintaining or developing resources that really don't fit your needs any more or serve you well. For example, you've been using your energy in ways that are more out of habit than out of desire. You may want to experiment with gradually shifting your use of resources, and make certain that you really want to discard them before you do.

Sneak Preview of Your Informational Interview

This exercise section is designed to help you create a list of questions that you can use to gather the career information most pertinent to your preferences and personality. Below are several prepared questions, along with space for you to write any additional questions that you may have. Read through the questions and transfer those most applicable to you to the informational interview compilation list at the end of Chapter 9. Feel free to ask students, family, and friends these questions to help you ascertain what is most important.

1. What kinds of resources does this job require?

2. What resources get heavily used?

3. What resources does this job provide?

4. What limitations would make it difficult to do this job?

5. How would this work impact _____ (fill in any special concern)?

Include your additional personalized questions here:

6.

7.

8.

FOCUS ON RESOURCES

Looking Within

Write as many endings to each sentence as you can.

1. The resources I'd most like to use are . . .

2. The resources I'd like to gain from my career are . . .

3. My career could impact my special concern by...

4. Resources that I want to protect are ...

Exploring Resources Associated with Careers

Based on your career options research, what's your best guess of the financial and energy resources associated with your top five career choices? List each career option. Beside each option, list each financial and energy resource in the column that best describes how you feel about needing and using that resource. You can determine the accuracy of your resource list once you've done the informational interviews.

Career Option	Financial and Energy Resources		
	Very Good Fit	Adequate Fit	Unacceptable Fit
1.			
2.			
3.			
4.			
5.			

Also, make your best guess about how your special concerns fit the five career options.

	Special Concerns		
Career Option	Very Good Fit	Adequate Fit	Unacceptable Fit
1.			
2.			
3.			
4.			
5.			

Wedge Work

Figure 6.1 shows an On Target model with Financial Resources, Energy Resources, and Special Concerns (Geographical Preference) wedges containing some sample entries. You can use these samples to get an idea of how filling in these wedges works. Earlier in this chapter you made some lists of your personal financial resources, your energy resources (time and emotional), and your special concerns. Now you need to place your list of financial resources in either the blank Survival Financial Resources wedge, as shown in Figure 6.2, or the Growth Financial Resources wedge, as shown in Figure 6.3. Next, you need to place your list of energy resources in either the blank Survival Energy Resources wedge, as shown in Figure 6.4, or the Growth Energy Resources wedge, as shown in Figure 6.5. Finally, you place your list of special concerns in either the blank Survival Special Concerns wedge, as shown in Figure 6.6, or the Growth Special Concerns wedge, as shown in Figure 6.7. To remind yourself of the distinctions between Growth and Survival modes, see Chapter 1.

In the Very Good Fit innermost sections of each wedge, list the words that represent the financial resources, energy resources, and special concerns you consider essential to express in your work. In the Adequate Fit middle sections, list words that reflect financial resources, energy resources, and special concerns you'd like to express in your work, those that would enhance the quality of your life but that aren't essential. In the Unacceptable Fit outer section, jot down those financial resources, energy resources, and special concerns that you would not want present in your work, those that would make doing your work nearly impossible.

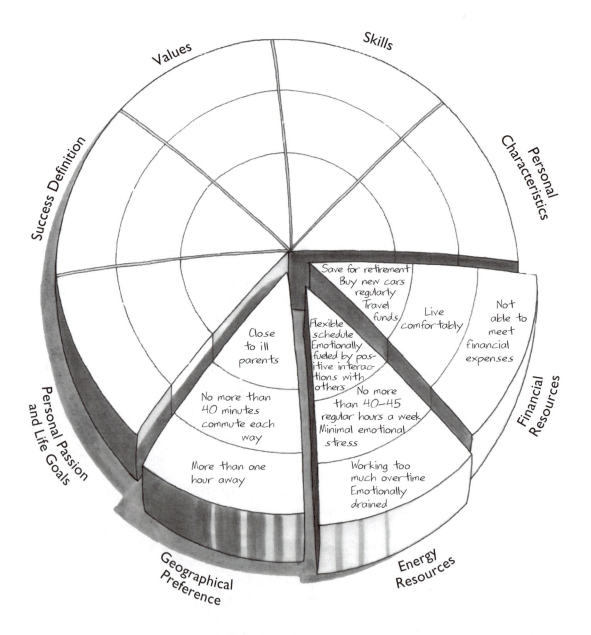

FIGURE 6.1   An On Target model with the *Financial Resources* and *Energy Resources* wedges completed with sample resources and a *Special Concerns* wedge labeled Geographical Preference filled in with some sample concerns.

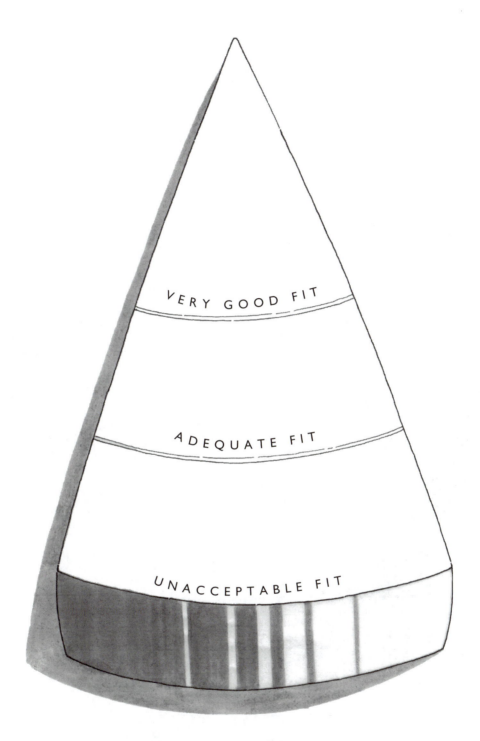

FIGURE 6.2 A blank *Survival Financial Resources* wedge, ready for you to fill in with words that describe your financial resources.

VERY GOOD FIT

ADEQUATE FIT

UNACCEPTABLE FIT

FIGURE 6.3   A blank *Growth Financial Resources* wedge, ready for you to fill in with words that describe your financial resources.

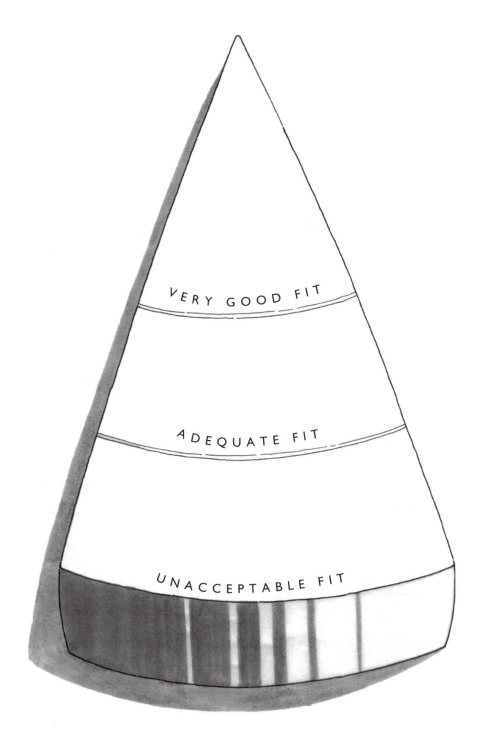

VERY GOOD FIT

ADEQUATE FIT

UNACCEPTABLE FIT

FIGURE 6.4 A blank *Survival Energy Resources* wedge, ready for you to fill in with words that describe your time and energy resources.

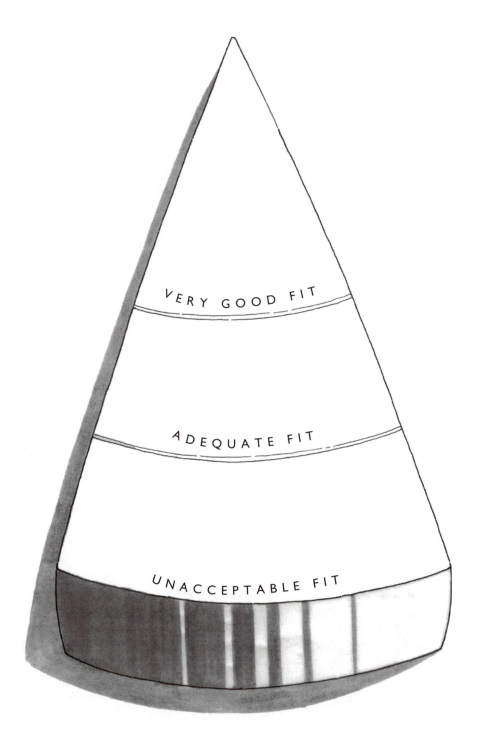

VERY GOOD FIT

ADEQUATE FIT

UNACCEPTABLE FIT

FIGURE 6.5   A blank *Growth Energy Resources* wedge, ready for you to fill in with words that describe your time and energy resources.

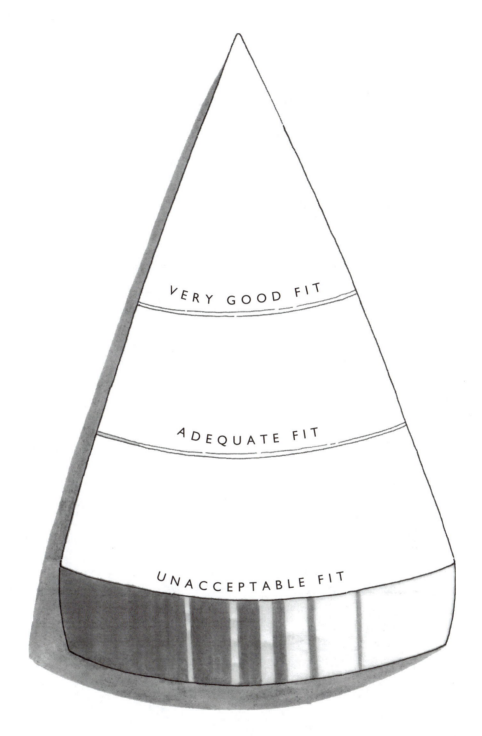

VERY GOOD FIT

ADEQUATE FIT

UNACCEPTABLE FIT

FIGURE 6.6   A blank *Survival Special Concerns* wedge, ready for you to label and fill in with words that describe your special concerns.

VERY GOOD FIT

ADEQUATE FIT

UNACCEPTABLE FIT

FIGURE 6.7   A blank *Growth Special Concerns* wedge, ready for you to label and fill in with words that describe your special concerns.

Once you have a sense that you have gathered all the essential resource-related information about yourself onto the enlarged Financial, Energy, and Special Concern wedges, you can transfer that information to your growth and survival copies of the On Target model in Chapter 8.

Consider These Questions...

1. What have you learned about the resources you need a career to provide?

2. What are your limitations or special considerations in choosing a career?

3. How might these limitations or special considerations shape your career options?

Ideas for Action

Use this space to write down thoughts, leads, ideas, and questions that you want to pursue.

Things to explore now   *Things to explore later*

RECOMMENDED READING

Allenbaugh, Eric. *Wake-Up Calls*. New York: Simon and Schuster, 1992.
Explores how to "complete" the areas in your life that are incomplete by recognizing your personal gaps, taking responsibility for them, and taking action to change them.

Robbins, Anthony. *Giant Steps*. New York: Fireside, 1994.
Offers simple, daily exercises to reduce limitations and increase personal, financial, and professional resources.

Sills, Judith. *Excess Baggage*. New York: Viking, 1993.
Explores common obstacles people create that prevent them from living satisfying lives and suggests ways to remove these obstacles.

7

FINDING YOUR SPARK
Personal Passion and Life Purpose

The purpose of this chapter is to assist you in uncovering or discovering your sense of aliveness and satisfaction—to help you find that internal spark or flash that allows you to feel actively engaged and passionately connected to the details and activities of your life.

The notion of aliveness is best looked at by answering the following questions. You can place your answers in the spaces provided.

What causes me to feel most alive?

In what moments have I felt most vibrant, the most connected to the world, the most expansive, the most alive?

What is my definition of aliveness?

ALIVENESS AND YOUR CAREER CHOICE

Aliveness is more than interests. You can have interests, be involved, and be curious without feeling passion and aliveness. Many career approaches focus on linking your interests with potential job options, yet fail to acknowledge that you can only be interested in what you are already aware of and have been exposed to, which can be limited by gender roles and cultural background.

If Teresa is asked, "Are you interested in repairing car engines?" she may very well answer "no" if she has had no exposure to engines or tools. If Teresa is asked, "What causes you to feel most alive?" she may well answer, "The ability to be self-sufficient, to solve problems, to master tasks, and fix things." Knowing what causes her to feel most alive, Teresa can begin to explore the array of jobs that involve solving problems and fixing things and may decide to investigate careers outside of her obvious interests.

Aliveness and satisfaction are crucial to the career-change process, because most of us have been engaged in work-related tasks that, for whatever reason, didn't tap into our sense of passion. These activities may have felt mundane or draining and may have sapped the very part of us that we rely on to feel alive and engaged with the world.

Answering the following questions can help uncover what would satisfy you in a career.

Ask yourself, "What would I do if I could get paid for anything?"

If someone said to you, "I will pay you $50,000 a year for doing any kind of productive work," what would you choose?

Now ask yourself, "What am I naturally drawn to, that I don't have to talk myself into, that I feel a natural pull toward, that I feel a real desire to pursue?"

I think of aliveness as enthusiasm, as a zest for pursuits, experiences, feelings, and activities. When you feel alive, you feel the spark of additional energy that snowballs and gives you energy to do more and creates more aliveness. Aliveness engenders a wonderful nonvicious cycle of creating more and more aliveness.

I think of satisfaction as a bit quieter and perhaps not as overtly active or visible as aliveness. Satisfaction is contentment, a sense of solid pleasure and fulfillment. You may need to experiment, to sample different life experiences or situations to find out what triggers the sense of aliveness, passion, and excitement that leads to ongoing satisfaction for you.

Aliveness, like the other qualities that we've examined, is determined by your individual style. One person's sense of aliveness may be active and high energy, and another's might be quiet and serene. What you're experiencing internally as a sense of aliveness or energy for what you're doing becomes your definition of aliveness, whether or not it parallels that of anyone else.

It's a challenge to be true to what really works and not to get hung up on, "Well, this seems like a strange thing to feel passionate about, but I do." Our passions are part of what makes our lives work, if we can find a way to incorporate them into our daily lives.

What if you don't have an inkling about what triggers your sense of aliveness and satisfaction? How do you uncover it if you can't find even the smallest hint of what causes you to feel alive? One way to learn what triggers aliveness in you is to look at what you feel hungry for in your life. What do you desire, crave, long for, want more of? What are you most hungry to create, pursue, experience, and feel? Are you hungry for the opportunity to have a voice in the world, to make a difference? Are you hungry for the ability to impact others, to be respected, or to be connected to others or to something bigger than yourself? Write your answers in the spaces below.

1.

2.

3.

4.

5.

6.

7.

8.

9.

10.

Whatever you feel most hungry for is what you need to pay attention to and try to incorporate into your personal and professional life.

Once you identify your hungers, you can use them to guide you to what nourishes and sustains your sense of aliveness.

CREATING A LIFE PHILOSOPHY

One way to capture your sense of aliveness is to create a life philosophy on paper. You can use this written record as a compass to guide you through important decisions. In a bit, I'll provide you with some questions that you can answer to help you shape your life philosophy. Add your own insights and responses to any issues not addressed by these questions—they are just a springboard to get you started.

Writing a life philosophy may seem like an extra task, especially if you're in the middle of trying to do a high-speed career change. You may think, "This isn't going to help me figure out what job I want or get my resumé done." Despite your feelings to the contrary, I advise you to write it because the time you put into writing it and the results you'll reap will benefit you immensely in your job search process. Your life philosophy can clarify your career-change process because it pulls together so much of what we've covered regarding your values, your skills, how you see yourself, what you're here to contribute, and what inspires you. Having a concise, written record often helps point you toward certain paths and choices and away from others.

Also, when things feel out of control, your written life philosophy can serve as a way of dropping anchor, of marking where you are. Your life philosophy won't stay static—it will change and evolve as you do. Don't look at it as the final statement of who you are and will forevermore be; it is just a picture of who you are at this moment in time.

Your life philosophy is the reason you grapple with the mundane day-to-day details of life. It can keep you focused or help you refocus on the bigger picture of what you want to accomplish. Although you may be in the middle of a retraining process or a tough work project, your life philosophy is a reminder that life isn't merely the momentary annoying details or troublesome, irritating tasks. Instead, these tasks and details contribute to your larger life vision.

Even with your life philosophy in hand, you may find the details and tasks of your life are several steps from your larger life vision. Here, it becomes especially important not to get discouraged. For example, you believe you're here to contribute to a world in which people are free to grow and develop their potential. You've decided to volunteer on a committee dedicated to improving livability in your neighborhood. The following week your work schedule is unexpectedly changed, making it impossible to attend the committee meetings. If you are focused only on attending those specific meetings, you might ask, "Why is this happening to me?" If you can step back and see the frustrating problem as a small detour to your larger goals, you can keep a perspective that allows you to stay focused on what is really meaningful to you.

Writing down a life philosophy and using it as a guiding beacon through day-to-day existence allows you to stay in touch with your passion and aliveness and that, in turn, creates a greater sense of satisfaction. Here are some questions to consider in writing your life philosophy:

1. Who am I and who am I becoming?

2. What motivates and inspires me?

3. What is my life purpose—what am I here to contribute?

4. What kind of world do I want to live in?

5. What will I do to leave the world a better place?

6. What will allow me to feel successful?

7. What people do I want to include in my life?

8. What kind of experiences do I want to seek?

9. How could my work help me feel satisfied and alive?

Using the information you glean from responding to these questions, write a concise statement of your life philosophy. Post it or key phrases from it in conspicuous locations where you can be reminded of it daily, especially when life is extra challenging.

TRANSLATING PASSION AND PHILOSOPHY INTO YOUR WORK

Even if you decided to forego writing out a life philosophy, take a moment and jot down a few keywords for each pertinent question. Look at those words now as we talk about how you can translate your personal sense of passion and your life philosophy into your work.

In a television interview, George Burns once said, "I'd rather fail at something I love than succeed at something I hate." I believe part of what he was speaking about is the importance of finding passion and purpose in your work. That's a much more straightforward task for some people than for others. It largely depends on whether your career choice occurs during a survival phase or a growth phase. If it occurs during a growth phase, chances are that it naturally follows what you feel passionate about.

If, however, it occurs during a survival phase, your challenge may be to find ways that you can feel bits of passion and aliveness from the work you do. In this case, you may need to look at how your job contributes to the bigger picture or see your job as a stepping stone to something you will be able to do later that will mesh better with your sense of passion and life purpose.

If you're working in a job that's far from your ideal and finding any genuine sense of passion and purpose in the work you're doing seems impossible, it's especially important to look at creating passion or aliveness in your personal and leisure life.

For example, if you're a human services–oriented person and you find yourself in an accounting job that you need to do for a while for survival reasons, ask yourself, Is there a way I can volunteer some accounting services for a nonprofit agency that serves a cause I believe in? Perhaps you can carve out five hours a week and volunteer it toward something that taps into your passion and life purpose.

Can you take a class that will lead to doing what you care most about? It's essential to find ways to tap into your passion, even if most of your work consists of survival-based activities. Find the spark of your passion and nurture it; fan your internal pilot light until your passion can be more central in your life.

Translating your personal passion and life goals into your work means finding its larger purpose and linking it to what's important to you. You can then say, "This is why I'm doing this. This is why it makes sense to me." If what you do feels meaningful, if it relates in some way to what you value and deem important, you can derive much more satisfaction and fulfillment.

Sneak Preview of Your Informational Interview

This exercise section is designed to help you create a list of questions that you can use to gather the career information most pertinent to your preferences and personality. Below are several prepared questions, along with space for you to write any additional questions. Read through the questions and transfer those that are most applicable to you to the informational interview compilation list at the end of Chapter 9. Feel free to practice asking students, family, and friends these questions to help you ascertain what is most important to you.

1. What do you find satisfying about this job?

2. How does this job contribute to your quality of life?

3. How does this job relate to what you feel most passionate about?

4. What motivates you to do this work?

5. This is what I feel most passionate about: _____. How might this job relate to that?

Include your additional personalized questions here:

6.

7.

8.

Focus on Personal Passion and Life Goals

Looking Within

Write as many endings to each sentence as you can.

1. For me, aliveness is…

2. Satisfaction means…

3. I feel most passionate about…

4. My most important life goals…

Exploring Personal Passion and Life Goals Associated with Careers

Based on your career options research, what's your best guess of the passion and life goals expressed and supported in your top five career options? List each career option. Beside each option, list each associated passion and life goal in the column that best describes how you feel about it. You can determine the accuracy of your personal passion and life goals list once you've done the informational interviews.

Career Option	Personal Passion and Life Goals		
	Very Good Fit	Adequate Fit	Unacceptable Fit
1.			
2.			
3.			
4.			
5.			

Updating Career Options

Consult your list of career options from Chapter 4, "Exploring Career Options." What level of aliveness do you feel as you consider each option? Are there any that you feel a strong desire to pursue, that you feel naturally drawn to? Which careers fit into that category for you?

Refer to your answers regarding aliveness and what you would do if you could get paid for anything. Did any new career options emerge from your answers? Take your responses to your school or local library or career center and ask for assistance in generating additional careers from the information in your responses. You can ask questions such as: Which careers would pay me for reading? What fields employ people who like to fix things?

Ask for information about these careers, and see if you can obtain written descriptions of the work, and what experiences are involved. Did what you learn change your top five career options? Did you discover related careers that looked appealing?

Write your updated career list here:

1.

2.

3.

4.

5.

Wedge Work

Figure 7.1 shows an On Target model with the Personal Passion and Life Goals wedge containing some sample passions and goals. You can use these samples to get an idea of how filling in these wedges works. Earlier in this chapter, you made several lists of your own passions and goals. Now you want to place these in either the blank Survival Personal Passion and Life Goals wedge, as shown in Figure 7.2, or the Growth Personal Passion and Life Goals wedge, as shown in Figure 7.3. To remind yourself of the distinctions between Growth and Survival modes, see Chapter 1.

In the Very Good Fit innermost section of each wedge, list the words that represent the personal passions and life goals you consider essential to express in your work. In the Adequate Fit middle section, list words that reflect personal passions and life goals you'd like to express in your work, those that would enhance the quality of your life but that aren't essential. In the Unacceptable Fit outer section, jot down those personal passions and life goals that you would not want present in your work, those that would make doing your work nearly impossible.

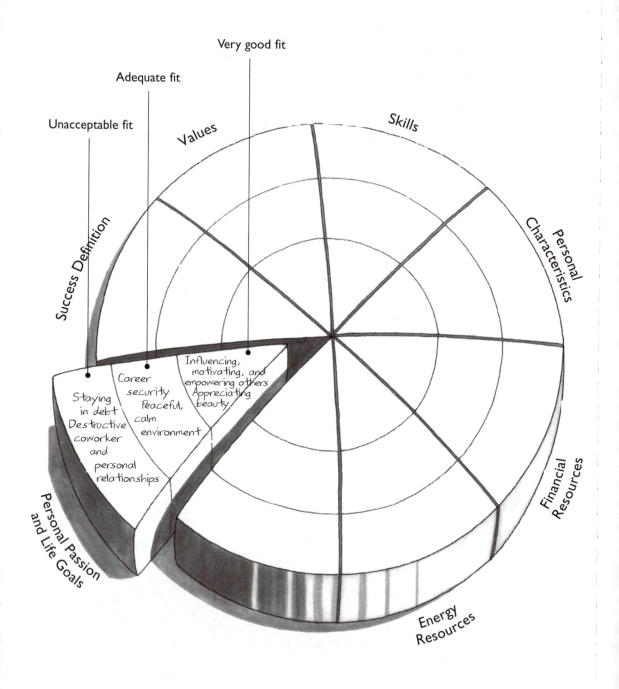

FIGURE 7.1   An On Target model, with the *Personal Passion and Life Goals* wedge filled in with sample passions and goals.

FIGURE 7.2 A blank *Survival Personal Passion and Life Goals* wedge, ready for you to fill in with words that describe your passions and goals.

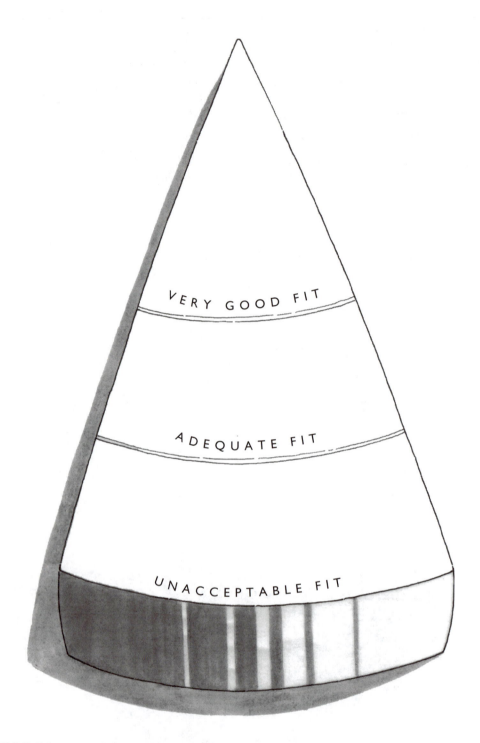

FIGURE 7.3 A blank *Growth Personal Passion and Life Goals* wedge, ready for you to fill in with words that describe passions you want to express and goals you want to work toward.

Once you have a sense that you have gathered all the essential information about yourself onto the enlarged passion and life goals wedge, you can then transfer that information to your growth and survival copies of the On Target model in Chapter 8.

Consider These Questions...

1. What have you learned about your definition of aliveness?

2. What can you do to help sustain your feelings of passion regarding your work?

3. What are the most important aspects of your sense of larger purpose and/or your life goals?

Ideas for Action

Use this space to write down thoughts, leads, ideas, and questions that you want to pursue.

Things to explore now   *Things to explore later*

RECOMMENDED READING

Anderson, Nancy. *Work With Passion.* New York: Carroll and Graf, 1984.
Lists the fears that prevent people from seeking passion in their lives and discusses the nine "passion secrets" that will help you lead a fulfilling life.

Seligman, Martin. *Learned Optimism.* New York: Simon and Schuster, 1990.
Offers tests to assess your current level of pessimism or optimism and how it influences your life. Assists in helping you learn to be more optimistic.

Wieder, Marcia. *Making Your Dreams Come True.* New York: Mastermedia, 1993.
Provides exercises, real life stories, and a personal workbook to allow you to become clear about your desires and to develop strategies for achieving them.

8

MAKING YOUR MARK
···
Creating a Personal Success Definition

DEFINING PERSONAL SUCCESS

Definitions of success are as varied as individuals and their differing values. Success might be a life with lots of freedom or lots of security. It might be a life with variety and challenge or with peace, constancy, and steadiness. Success can be internally defined as feeling good about yourself and your activities. Success can be externally defined as others' viewing what you do or who you are in a positive way.

Recognizing Family Influences

Your personal definition of success comes in part from family attitudes and beliefs about success. In Chapter 3 we talked about family influences and the shaping of values. In some families, success is a value to be sought after; others have an unspoken rule that success is somehow a betrayal of the family system. These families may believe that no one in the family should surpass anyone else and may consider success an act of abandonment or betrayal. Within that kind of family system, success could mean money, power, professional status, an expensive home, or getting to do exactly what you want to do when you want to do it.

Because your definition of success comes in part from your family's attitudes and beliefs about success, it may even be a direct reflection of the messages you received growing up. You may find that you partially replay those early messages and follow most of your family's notion of success but alter it in some significant way. Conversely, you may see your definition of success as an absolute rejection of your family's definition.

Your definition of success may have been unconsciously shaped by some of these notions: Women are not supposed to be as successful as men; the only successful job is one you have for 40 years; success is doing a job in which you produce something concrete and useful. Despite these unconscious shapings, you believe that success is doing a job that you love, that you'll only do it for 10 years, and that it doesn't produce something concrete. Suddenly, your sense of success is at odds with what you were taught, creating internal conflicts that can cause you to feel guilty or confused.

Having a Success Mentor

Another way to explore your vision of success is to examine the lives of people you admire and consider successful. What is it about those people or their lives that strikes you as successful? What are they doing or not doing? How have they managed to shape their lives that causes you to view them as successful? Ask yourself: "How can I emulate those people? How can I draw on what they do and incorporate some of their success into my life?"

Just as we may often select a mentor to assist us on the job site or to help us develop a new aspect of our lives, we can choose a success mentor. Because we consider this person successful, we can ask for her assistance, support, guidance, and knowledge in learning how to do the same for ourselves.

Selecting a success mentor does not mean molding ourselves into a carbon copy of that person's success. Rather it may mean learning how our mentor transforms wishes, hopes, dreams, and longings into actuality, whether those are experiences, material possessions, or qualities such as freedom, independence, security, or connection. Having a mentor means learning her process, not necessarily the particulars of what she's done in her situation.

Someone who has a history of being successful has usually learned a process that can often help other people. You can follow the steps and start to learn the process for yourself. You may need to experiment, delete what doesn't work for you, and add steps that meet your needs more fully.

Writing Your Own Definition

Defining personal success is going to be mitigated by whether you're in a survival stage or a growth stage. If you're in survival mode, success may mean paying the rent, putting food on everyone's plate, and holding a job in a tight economy. That's very different from being in growth mode and having the luxury of asking questions such as, Do I enjoy my job? Does it fulfill me?

In a growth phase, your definition of success may be very different from your definition of success in a survival phase. When you are focused on surviving, it can be a luxury to say, "I would like a lot of independence and personal freedom in my life and my job." Survival may necessitate that you have a job with an immense amount of supervision, even though it does not remotely reflect your definition of success. Sometimes what you do in the short run may not align with your long-term notion of success.

If you are in this situation, I encourage you to write two definitions of success: a For Now definition, and a Big Picture definition. Your For Now definition might focus on moving toward future goals, making gradual yet steady progress toward what is important to you, and meeting your life responsibilities in an adequate and reliable way.

My For Now success definition:

Your Big Picture definition of success should focus on what you want when you have the time and means to create it for yourself and describe what you are ultimately moving toward, even as you attend to survival needs in the moment. This statement should honestly reflect what feels most important to you. Try not to worry about whether people will respect you or what they'll think if they know you really want material things. Often, people worry that others will view them as shallow if their definition of success means buying a car with air conditioning rather than creating world peace.

My Big Picture success definition:

Be scrupulously honest with yourself about your definition of success. You never have to show it to anyone or discuss it, but you need to be clear in your head about what genuinely is important to you. If you try to fool yourself into believing something that isn't true for you, you're going to be perpetually dissatisfied and not understand why you're so unhappy when you've achieved what you were *supposed* to want.

If you don't feel comfortable sharing that with others, if you feel some need to appear differently than you are to others, that's your business. What will get you into deep trouble is deceiving yourself about what's actually important to you. Defining success is not about winning bonus points from people. It's about you getting to live a life full of satisfaction and personal richness, because what you've created for yourself aligns with what you've held as highly valuable and important.

There's nothing wrong with valuing material things, although that's usually the place where most people feel shame about their definition of success. They don't tend to feel shame about wanting to help others, wanting personal freedom, and the like. The definitions of success that create the most shame for people include wanting certain material things, wanting not to have to work very hard or do very much, and longing to be taken care of by some other person or have a very high paying job.

It's important to separate your ideal fantasy scenario from your realistic definition of success. Depending on other people for our definition of success sets us up for failure, for rampant disappointment, and for possible abuse. If someone else controls whether we experience success and satisfaction in our lives, we are in deep trouble should they change their minds about what they're doing, stop all together, or redefine success for themselves.

Your definition and achievement of success needs to come from your own energies and actions. If you feel a huge discrepancy between your definition of success and your ability to create it, look at the components that cause the chasm. You may find it helpful to consult a therapist or a career counselor, looking at what may be causing the chasm and what else might be at work in the situation.

EXPLORING AND OVERCOMING BARRIERS TO SUCCESS

Barriers Can Be Internal or External

Barriers to success can be internal or external. Examples of external barriers are not enough money to get additional training or to relocate to an area that is better for your career, having people actively thwart you, or needing a long history of work experience to get a job in a field. You may or may not have immediate control over external barriers to success.

An example of an internal barrier to success is self-doubt: despite evidence to the contrary, you believe that you can't make it, that it's too hard to achieve or create what you want. You sabotage yourself before you start, or as you start to make progress, you inadvertently start to question if you're doing the right thing. Self-sabotage can also occur when you really are making it. If it's too threatening to someone else in your life, you can unconsciously impair your ability to continue succeeding. An internal barrier to success can be a bad habit such as being late, being forgetful, or failing to be assertive.

With some work and diligence you can diminish or remove internal barriers to success.

Other barriers to success can be a mixture of the internal and the external barriers. For example, your family model dictates that nobody in the family is allowed to be substantially more successful than anyone else. Or your parents see themselves as highly unsuccessful; your personal success feels like betrayal and abandonment.

You express that form of loyalty by holding yourself back; the implication is if you can do it, perhaps they could have done it. Another implication is that you're somehow experiencing something that they didn't get a chance to experience, and it's unkind for you to do that because it will just remind them of everything they didn't get to do.

Challenge that belief system; your success does not take away from anyone else. It is not as though there is a big blackberry pie of success and that there are only so many pieces to go around. It's possible for everyone to be successful; your success in the here and now does not diminish someone else's possibilities. Nor is it the cause or the source of another person's feelings of inadequacy or discomfort. Those negative feelings are already in place; and although your success may trigger or intensify those feelings, you did not create them.

The more we strive to live up to our highest desires and potentials, the more we benefit. Stifling your talents and desires to help others not feel badly about themselves results in a huge loss that in turn creates another generation of children growing to adulthood with conflicting feelings about pursuing what is important to them.

In addition, be on the alert for the use of "yes, but . . ." in conversation and thought, both from yourself and others. "Yes, but . . ." can often point toward barriers that you may not be fully conscious of possessing. Someone says to you, "Why don't you just move to Tulsa and take that printing job? They're offering everything you want." And you say "Yes, it's everything I ever wanted, but I'm worried about what will happen if I'm in a new city." Whatever follows that "but" is usually a barrier to your success. In this case it might be fear of the unknown, of being in a new city and separated from family and friends. It might be fear of making a change or fear of leaving a job that, as unsatisfactory as it might be, is safe, known, and secure. It might mean fear of new challenges and learning new things. These fears can be huge barriers to success.

Challenge Your Worries, Concerns, and Fears

Another clue to barriers to success is to look at what you tend to catastrophize about. What are your biggest worries, concerns or fears? Many times we create self-imposed barriers out of the things we catastrophize about. Here's an example: If I really go for success, people aren't going to want to be around me. I'm going to lose friends, or people will stop taking care of me if I'm really successful because I'll look like I don't need anything.

Challenge those worries by asking: "Will you like me less if I'm successful? Will you be less inclined to give me nurturing and care if I achieve and am successful?" What if the answer is: "No, it's not a problem. Go for it." You do exactly that and your worst nightmare comes true: They pull back, or they're not available, or they withhold their nurturing.

If that occurs, you've learned an important lesson: Relationship disruptions can occur when others feel threatened or jealous of your achievements. You don't have to give up on the notion of going after your own personal definition of success. You do need to have discussions with the important people in your life and say "I'm feeling deeply concerned about this—you supported my pursuit of what's important to me, and now I sense that you're pulling away from the relationship."

You may find out that the relationship disruption is merely coincidence. The shift in behavior may be related to personal issues in that other person's life. If it is related to your pursuit of success, the next step is to sit down and negotiate with the person and say, "Is there something you need from me, some kind of reassurance or behavior that would allow you to feel more comfortable with this and feel less threatened and more supportive?" You may find that he simply needs some reassurance that as you move forward with your life, he won't be left behind. Try to spend more time with him and include him in your new activities.

You may find that someone simply doesn't like your growth and your pursuit of what's important to you. She may see an either/or situation—either you can attend to her comfort level and not change, or you're choosing growing over her. That dilemma can be painful to resolve. You may be held hostage to the demand of not growing to sustain another person's comfort level. It is very difficult, if not impossible, to have someone in your life who has the attitude that any growth, self-initiated action, or pursuit takes something away from him. Look closely at the dynamics of any such relationship because a time will most likely come when you feel growth is essential to your well-being. Not to honor that takes away from yourself and from what you can contribute to the world.

Tap into Your Resources

You can often diminish or eliminate barriers by tapping into or developing your resources. For example, Martina is frustrated because what she wants to do next requires money that she lacks. By developing her resources and looking at how she can either cut down on her expenses or generate more income, she's on the path to reducing a barrier to success. Personal resources work the same way.

For example, Leon goes into self-doubt a good deal of the time. He can remove that barrier by starting to take more risks and by trying to tune out the self-doubt chatter in his head. As he makes more good decisions and has situations work out well, he can start arguing with that self-doubt: Despite my self-doubt, look how well things turned out. He can also look at the qualities he values in himself and explore how he can mobilize them to help reduce or eliminate those barriers. Be realistic and clear about your barriers, however. You don't want to say, "I'm not going to worry about them" or "They're not that big" when indeed they are fairly significant.

By the same token, don't be too self-limiting. Avoid saying, "I have these barriers, and it will take me forever to get rid of them. So what's the point?" The point is, if you chip away at them a bit at a time, you will diminish them.

I always think of a large rock in a small stream; that rock is a barrier to the water moving down the stream. Even though the rock slows the movement of the water, the entire rock does not need to be out of the way for the water to flow. The water can start to flow over the rock; and as it does, it slowly starts to reduce the rock's size. Water can start to flow around the edge of the rock and through cracks in the rock. You do not have to wait until a barrier disappears to go forward and create success in your life.

CREATING SUCCESS IN YOUR WORK

Creating success in your work may look different from creating success in your personal life. What is in the Big Picture of success in your day-to-day life? What kind of relationships do you want? What kind of setting do you want to live in? What experiences do you want? You may find that your work definition of success is different from your personal definition of success.

Part of my work definition of success is being able to assist people in growing, changing, and striving for what they want in ways that work for them and do not damage themselves or others. In my personal life, I don't find much desire to do that with people close to me. Certainly I want to be supportive, a good listener, and an ally in problem-solving, but if during my private life I did what I do in my work life, I would feel like the opposite of success.

A useful exercise is to compare your personal definition of success with your work definition of success. You may find a wonderful overlap or a near match, or you may find radical differences.

The more a person's work is his life, the more that alignment is present. What is important, however, is not the degree of alignment that's present in your life, but the degree of alignment that you need to feel satisfied. There's no right or wrong answer; the only consideration is your need. Otherwise, you can have a successful work life and be stumped about why you feel so dissatisfied. You may be trying to apply your work definition of success to your personal life even though it doesn't fit. It's okay for those definitions to be different as long as you can blend and weave them in an overall pattern that works well for you.

To create success in your work, you need to know the criteria that indicate success in that job or career. What an air traffic controller needs to do on the job to be successful may be radically different from what a dental hygienist or a veterinarian needs to do to be successful. You may be in survival mode and have a job that doesn't fit your overall definition of success; in the short run, however, it may be imperative to do that job, and you need to figure out a way to do that job in a successful manner.

An informational interview might be helpful. Ask someone performing that job, "What is important to be successful in this job?" The success elements may be tasks, talents, abilities, behaviors, certain ways of interacting with coworkers, or interacting with the public.

Often, one of the most important ways to create success on the job is the attitude you convey about the work you're doing. I've been around highly proficient people whose attitude toward their job is so negative that they convey the energy, mood, and tone of someone unsuccessful.

Attitude is crucial even if you're doing a job that does not fulfill your definition of success. If you're doing a job for survival sake, you can say, "This is important for me to do well, because every time I accomplish something with determination and attention to detail and do a good job of it, my sense of self-worth, accomplishment, and self-esteem increases, and that benefits everyone."

What kind of attitude do you need to develop and practice conveying? In addition to information and a good attitude, what do you need to feel successful in your job or career?

I once worked as a dishwasher in a barbecue restaurant. This job did not match my personal definition of success, nor did it meet any other important emotional needs. Yet I needed the job to fulfill some survival needs, such as paying rent. Since I knew I was going to be working that job for quite some time, success consisted of showing up on time, staying until the end of my shift, and making certain that I did what I needed to do during the course of my shift. That was my personal definition of success for that job situation. It was not that I made a deep connection with my boss, nor that I found some kind of hidden fulfillment in doing the dishes. None of that was there. What was there was that I showed up, I did my shift and I earned a paycheck that allowed me to meet my basic survival needs.

Another way to get a taste of what you need to be successful at a given job is to do what's called *shadowing*. Shadowing is contacting someone who is doing a job in a profession that you're interested in and literally being that person's shadow for a work day, seeing what she is called upon to do, what allows her to do her job well, and how she contributes to that process. What attitudes and interaction styles, personal qualities, tasks, and approaches does she incorporate to create success on the job? Later you can consider whether these match aspects of yourself—what you're willing and able to do.

Again, I cannot stress enough the importance of developing a success attitude, not just on the job, but in life in general. A success attitude says that I can do what I put my mind to, I can have the things I want, I can have the crucial aspects of my life, I can have fulfilling relationships, I can have work that suits and fits me well, and I can have a life that matches my picture of what I believe life is like when it's going well.

A success attitude is the mid-step between your definition of success and your experience of success. When you define success for yourself, you point your compass in the right direction—you know where you need to head—and your destination is the experience of that success daily. The vehicle that gets you there is your success attitude. It allows you to approach problems with zest and optimism saying, "I can do this, I'm going to do this, even if it takes me a while." You don't stop striving for what you want because you don't receive immediate gratification for your efforts. You believe in yourself, and in moments when your belief falters, you have people in your life who remind you of their belief in you.

Without a success attitude, you can have a definition of success, and you can infrequently experience moments of success in your life. But to end up experiencing ongoing personal and career success, you need a success attitude, because that's what keeps you on track.

FOCUS ON A SUCCESS DEFINITION

Looking Within

Write as many endings to each sentence as you can.

1. In my family, success meant...

2. The only ways for me to be successful are…

3. If I were to do exactly what I want…

4. If I weren't worried about other people's reactions, I'd…

Informational Interview Question List

This exercise section is designed to help you create a list of questions that you can use to gather the career information most pertinent to your preferences and personality. Below are several prepared questions, along with space for you to write any additional questions. Read through the questions below and transfer those that are most applicable to you to the informational interview compilation list at the end of Chapter 9. Try asking students, family, and friends these questions to help you ascertain what is most important to you.

1. What does it mean to be successful in this work?

2. How do you determine if you're successful?

3. What would prevent you from being successful in this career?

4. My definition of success is _____. How would that fit in this job?

Include your additional personalized questions here:

5.

6.

7.

Exploring Success Definitions Associated with Careers

Based on your career options research, what's your best guess of the definition of success in your top five career options? List each career option. Beside each option, list each definition of success in the column that best describes how you feel about that definition. You can determine the accuracy of your success definitions list once you've done the informational interviews.

	Definition of Success		
Career Option	Very Good Fit	Adequate Fit	Unacceptable Fit
1.			
2.			
3.			
4.			
5.			

Wedge Work

Figure 8.1 shows an On Target model with the Success Definition wedge containing some sample definitions of success. You can use these samples to get an idea of how filling in these wedges works. Earlier in this chapter, you made several lists of your own definitions of success. Now you want to place these in either the blank Survival Success Definition wedge, as shown in Figure 8.2, or the Growth Success Definition wedge, as shown in Figure 8.3. To remind yourself of the distinctions between Growth and Survival modes, see Chapter 1.

In the Very Good Fit innermost section of each wedge, list the words that represent the definitions of success you consider essential to express in your work. In the Adequate Fit middle section, list words that reflect definitions of success you'd like to express in your work, those that would enhance the quality of your life but that aren't essential. In the Unacceptable Fit outer section, jot down those definitions of success that you would not want present in your work, those that would make doing your work nearly impossible.

Once you have a sense that you have gathered *all* the essential information about yourself onto the enlarged success wedge, you can transfer that information to your growth and survival copies of the On Target model (Figures 8.4 and 8.5).

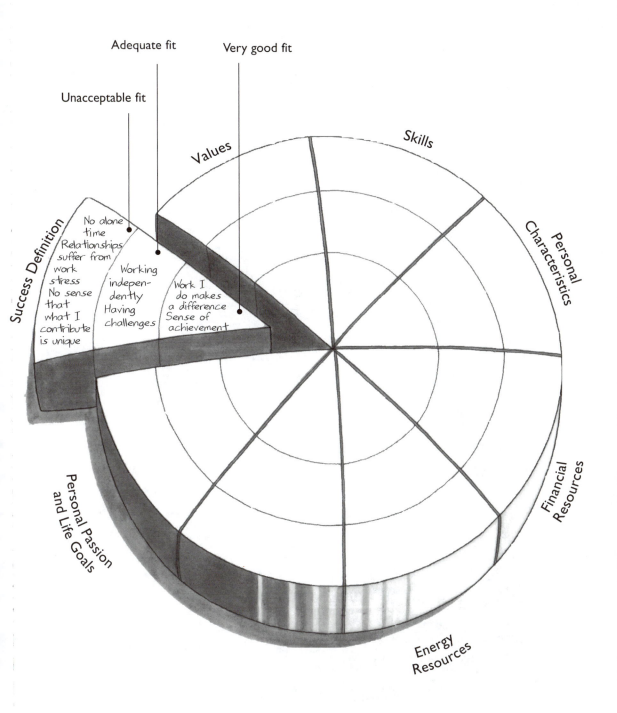

Adequate fit

Very good fit

Unacceptable fit

Values

Skills

Personal Characteristics

Success Definition

No alone time Relationships suffer from work stress No sense that what I contribute is unique

Working independently Having challenges

Work I do makes a difference Sense of achievement

Personal Passion and Life Goals

Financial Resources

Energy Resources

FIGURE 8.1   An On Target model, with the *Success Definition* wedge filled in with sample definitions of success.

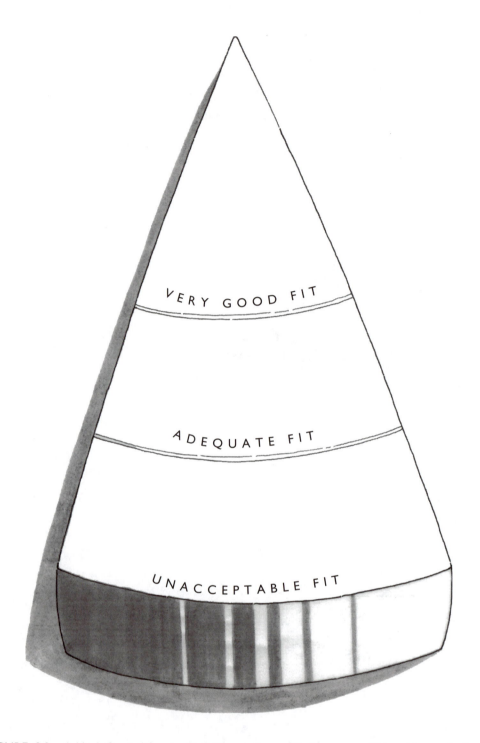

FIGURE 8.2 A blank *Survival Success Definition* wedge, ready for you to fill in with words that describe your definition of success in survival mode.

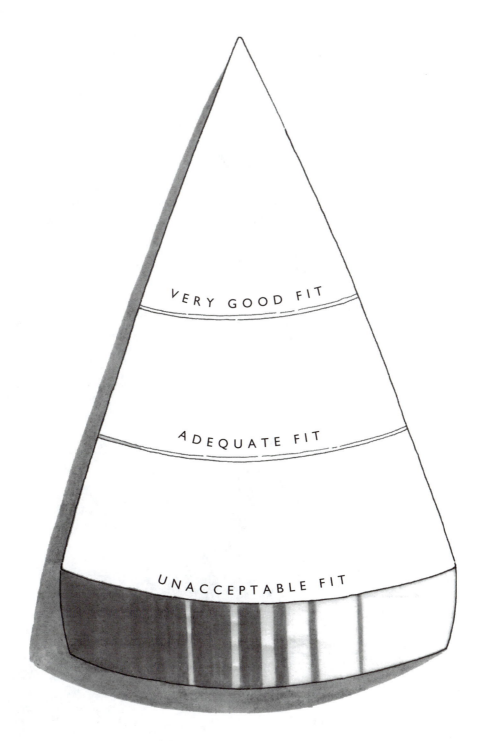

FIGURE 8.3 A blank *Growth Success Definition* wedge, ready for you to fill in words that describe your definition of success in growth mode.

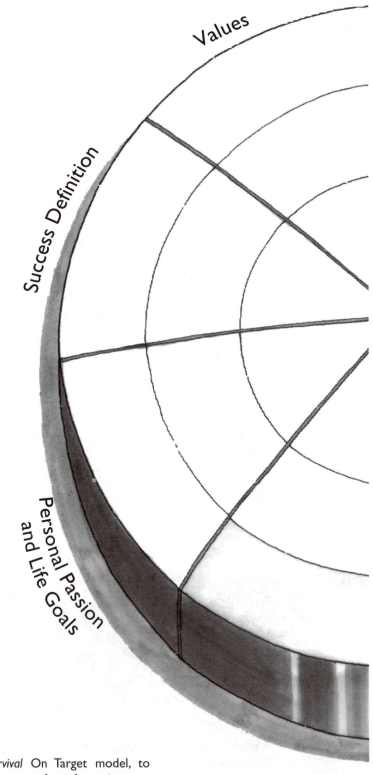

FIGURE 8.4 A blank *Survival* On Target model, to which you can transfer information you entered on the blank *Survival* wedges in this and previous chapters.

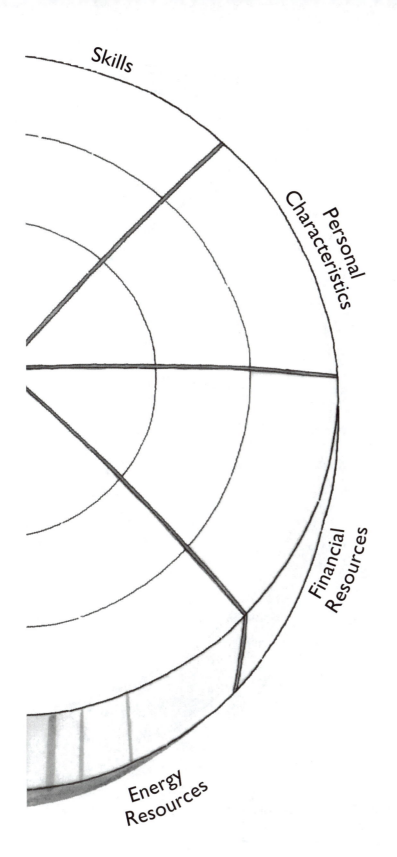

Skills

Personal Characteristics

Financial Resources

Energy Resources

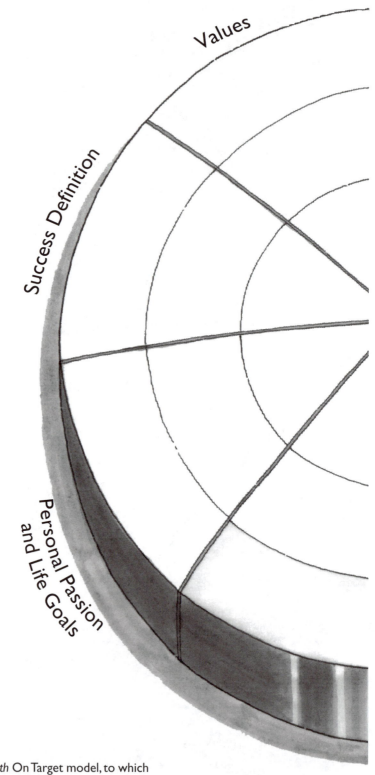

FIGURE 8.5 A blank *Growth* On Target model, to which you can transfer information you entered on the blank *Growth* wedges in this and previous chapters.

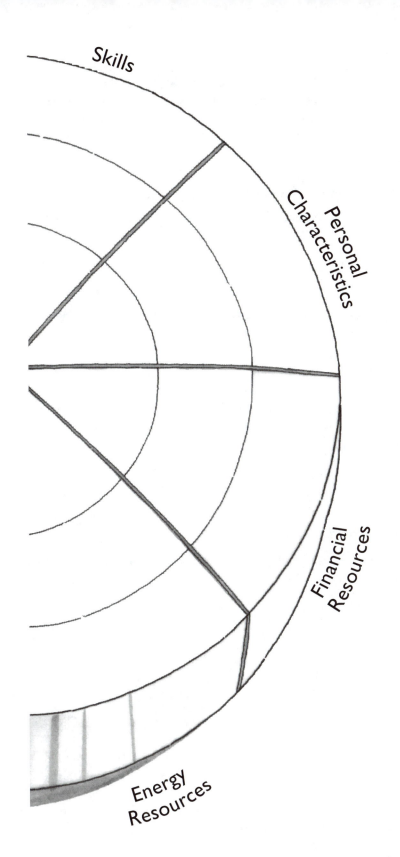

Skills

Personal
Characteristics

Financial
Resources

Energy
Resources

Congratulations! You have completed the On Target model. Now you should have a clearer picture of how a career can be congruent with you as an individual. Chapter 9 guides you through the next step: making a career decision. You will use the completed model in this step.

Consider These Questions...

1. What have you learned about your potential barriers to success?

2. What might help you minimize or overcome these barriers?

3. How do your current behaviors and beliefs contribute to a success attitude?

Ideas for Action

Use this space to write down thoughts, leads, ideas, and questions that you want to pursue.

Things to explore now   *Things to explore later*

RECOMMENDED READING

Helmstetter, Shad. *The Self-Talk Solution.* New York: Simon and Schuster, 1987.

Teaches how to reprogram negative inner dialogues with motivating self-talk. Assists with increasing self-confidence and optimism.

Jeffers, Susan. *Feel the Fear and Do It Anyway.* New York: Ballantine, 1987.

Presents techniques for managing fear and indecision while taking appropriate risks, for reducing negative self-talk, and for learning new ways to accomplish goals.

Sher, Barbara. *I Could Do Anything.* New York: Delacorte, 1994.

Provides exercises, motivational techniques, and practical advice for helping people reach clarity regarding their true career desires.

9

HEADS OR TAILS
Making Smart Decisions

What makes a decision a good decision? A bad decision? When in the decision-making process do you decide if a decision is good or bad? Immediately after you've made the decision? After you've received solicited or unsolicited feedback? Is a decision bad the moment something negative happens as a result of the decision? Is a decision bad once consequences you weren't expecting occur? Is a decision bad if it leads to any outcome other than the one that was most desirable for you? Is a decision good if you get exactly what you want and/or no one disapproves of you?

How long does a decision have to be right to be right for you? Often, in terms of the career process, people feel that the only "correct" career decision is a lifetime career decision. I ask you to consider the notion of a "lifetime" versus a "for now" decision in relation to future career choices. It's highly unlikely that a career decision will be a lifetime decision for most of us. Those of you who are in the process of changing careers for the first time may also be confronting that awareness for the first time. Others, more accustomed to changing career directions, already know that to be true.

If you can look at a career decision as a "for now" or "for the foreseeable future" decision, you may be able to let yourself off the hook of trying to choose a "perfect" career or make a perfect lifetime decision. Many of our parents or grandparents made a career decision in their youth and that was the career or job they had until retirement. Times have changed, and many of us can expect our jobs to become outmoded or replaced by technological advances, requiring us to shift careers or, at the very least, develop new job skills. Despite this knowledge, many of us still operate out of the old model that if at age 15 you decide you are going to be a firefighter for the rest of your life and something happens to disrupt that, something is wrong with you, you've done something incorrectly, or you've made a bad decision.

WHAT IS A BAD DECISION?

I define a bad decision as a decision that you don't learn anything from. The primary purpose of this book is to help you gather information that you can organize in a usable, discernible fashion so that you can make clear decisions about what to choose next. Once you gather all this information, though, it can become easy to freeze at the decision-making fork in the road, saying, "Okay, so I have all of this information, but how do I make a good decision? How do I make certain that I use this information wisely?"

First, promise yourself that you're not going to try to make a perfect decision. There is no such thing, because who you are keeps changing, so what would be a perfect decision in one moment will eventually no longer fit you. As you learned in Chapter 3, you continue to change and grow and your values also continue to change and grow. You may decide that you want to develop new skills, as discussed in Chapter 4, or you may get weary of using skills that are well-developed and want to develop others. Your sense of who you are and what you feel passionate about may shift and evolve over time. What feels like success at age 30 may not feel like success at age 50. For a variety of reasons, earlier decisions may have been solid and positive in that moment but may no longer be appropriate.

Second, consider that it is all right to change your mind. Obviously, this has ramifications if you're focusing on a career that requires a long training period, several years of school, financial expense during training or schooling, and diminished income because of time lost from the workplace or as a result of starting over in a new field. Consider your options carefully, wisely, and from all angles, but don't paralyze yourself by trying to dissect every possible angle and predict every potential outcome. It simply isn't possible. Give yourself permission to make a decision, to go forward with it, to change your mind if necessary, and to tell yourself that if the decision doesn't fit later or doesn't feel right, you'll give yourself permission to decide again.

Try to look at the decision-making process and classify decisions as "wise" or "unwise." Wise decisions are those you make with your eyes open, having gathered a reasonable amount of information and having created some kind of structure or format for sorting that information. In this book, the structure is completing the On Target model and then making your best choice. Consult reliable people whose judgment you trust, engage in conversations with objective professionals, look at what makes most sense for you at this point in your life, factor in which kind of decision-making model represents your current situation, and then make your choice and attempt to make it work for you. Unwise decisions are those you make without creating a model for sorting information; those for which you neglect to consider a certain area that you know is important, or those for which you gather information but throw it overboard, following someone's opinion about what you should do because you're concerned about losing approval or someone's time or focus.

The only other unwise decision is not deciding. Most of us engage in some of this not-deciding occasionally and say, "I don't know what I want to do tonight, I'll just get home and see what I feel like," and often end up watching television. That's not what I'm talking about. I'm talking about not-deciding as a way of letting fate or other people decide for you. That's still a decision; it's just a decision devoid of power, impact, and ability to create for yourself what you want.

Most of us also engage in small amounts of this via procrastination. It's normal to want to shy away from making decisions because often it feels as if—especially in the case of career decisions—the ramifications of making a choice, any choice, are going to be huge. And there's the potential future embarrassment of, "What if I change my mind? How am I going to deal with people saying, 'Well, I thought you wanted to go into the computer field, but now you're saying you want to go into the health care field. How did that happen? When are you going to make up your mind?'"

It's normal to shy away from making decisions, and it's also necessary to push through that resistance to make decisions. Don't let fate or others decide for you; acknowledge that you're going to do your utmost to make the best decision you know how with the information that you have at the time. People do not deliberately, consciously make horrible decisions. Often, we beat ourselves up emotionally down the road when we gain additional life experience, insight, awareness, or information. Usually, the information wasn't there before, or we didn't have the life experience or the awareness to recognize it for what it was and process it. Grant yourself the understanding and acceptance of the notion that you'll make the best decision you know how with the available information and that it is always better to choose consciously than to let your life happen to you.

You did not necessarily make a poor decision even though your decision did not turn out as you might have expected. This also does not mean that you can't trust your judgment, your instincts, or your decision-making abilities. Everyone makes decisions that they later feel don't turn out well. That's where the universal desire for a crystal ball comes from. If you could see the future, if you could see what was going to happen next, often it would have an impact on what you would choose to create or have happen next. We don't have that kind of foresight; so you make your best decision, and you prepare yourself for the foreseeable consequences—positive and negative—not knowing what might happen next.

ASSESSING YOUR RISK THRESHOLD

Part of not knowing what might happen next is dealing with your own personal risk level. Each person can handle a different amount of risk, and that amount varies according to a person's current life situation. At times, for example, a person can take risks because she is responsible only for herself. She may feel especially adventurous, rebellious, or emotionally resilient, and taking a risk feels very manageable.

Conversely, at other times parenting responsibilities, finances, ill health, or emotional fatigue may make taking risks seem impossible. In assessing your risk threshold, realize that in this particular moment you may need to play it safe, minimize your risks, and maximize your safety and security. And even though it may go against the grain of who you are, there may be a time when you can afford more risk in your life and in your decision making. Be honest with yourself about where you are right now because sometimes who we are and what we need to do do not perfectly mesh. You may be a very adventurous person, but if you're at a place in life where your health is challenged, you may not get to follow your true nature, and you may need to make different decisions than you would make in healthier times. You may be at a point in your life where your financial resources are limited and you can't afford to relocate to another state for training. You need to make a choice that takes those limits into consideration.

What an unacceptable level of risk is for you depends on your vulnerable areas. Do you feel at risk with your finances, health, personal relationships, or where you live? And where do you feel resilient, really sturdy, as if you can afford to take some risks? These areas of vulnerability usually change for people depending on their life stages and the specific circumstances of their life. It's another way of figuring out what you can gamble on and what you can't. Make a list of the things that you feel vulnerable about:

1.

2.

3.

4.

5.

6.

7.

8.

9.

10.

When you make a decision, do you focus mainly on how it will turn out, or on how others will feel about it and view it? Are you a decision-maker who focuses on fact and the information at hand, or do you focus on the feeling aspect, how you and others are going to feel and respond to the decision? Most of us look at our decisions from both standpoints—the facts and the feelings. Most of us lean in one direction or another, however, in terms of our comfort zone, in terms of where we are willing to accept more risk. If you feel at risk in your relationships, the feeling aspect of decision-making may carry more weight because you feel you have more to lose if people disapprove or if the decision jeopardizes your relationships.

Conversely, if you feel more at risk in terms of financial or time considerations, you may feel you can face the risk of others' disapproval because your relationships feel sturdy. Instead, you may feel more vulnerable to the potential financial risks of pursuing a career, such as salary and prospects for advancement.

You need to know whether you operate more out of feeling or fact when making decisions, but also to realize that this may change, depending on your life stage. After identifying whether fact or feeling tends to dominate your decision making, try to find someone whose judgment you trust to take the position opposite of yours, and debate the pros and cons to fill in any information gaps. It's a nice way to counterbalance whatever mode you might be in and a good way to double-check your thinking and feeling process.

If you focus on facts and outcomes, ask yourself how you make your decisions and how you decide what is acceptable and unacceptable. Do you focus on what might go wrong from the decision, or how perfect things might be, or do you go back and forth from one to the other? It's very important to find the middle ground between catastrophizing outcomes and idealizing them. You want that middle ground where you can imagine a decision in which you like some of the consequences but acknowledge that parts of it don't appeal to you.

If you focus on people and feelings rather than on outcomes and facts, do you also focus on people's approval or disapproval or some other aspect that will have an impact on their response or relationship with you? Do you focus on how a decision will win the love and approval of those around you or bring rejection and shame upon you? Again, look for the middle ground; try to envision a decision that some people feel positive about and others don't. Regardless of your decision-making style, resist thinking in black and white, in absolute terms. The truth usually lies somewhere between the two extremes.

FORK IN THE ROAD:
A DECISION-MAKING FRAMEWORK

Given your risk threshold and phase of life, what kind of decision do you need to make for yourself? Which decision-making fork you take for a particular decision will radically influence the information you take in and the way you process it.

As I said in Chapter 1, it's an excellent idea to do an On Target model for careers that are based on a survival mode and a growth mode. If for some reason, a career comes up equally well on both charts, that's a wonderful indicator that a career can meet both your survival and growth needs. However, that's extremely rare. One reason people feel confused about career choices as well as about general decision making is that they don't clarify the kind of decision they need to make. It's absolutely okay to consider safety and security when making survival decisions. Unless one's basic needs are met, it's nearly impossible to look at growth needs as anything but a luxury.

If you don't determine which road you need to take for a particular decision, you can end up doubling back repeatedly and confusing yourself by mixing two sets of information. You need to decide both where your risk threshold is and whether you can go for the brass ring. Is this the time you can make decisions based on growth and enrichment desires, or do you need to make decisions based on immediate survival concerns such as feeding the kids, paying rent, covering doctor bills, or being in the job market again as soon as possible? Or can you afford to take a bit more time, pursue options that might be more risky in terms of job opportunities or that might keep you out of the job market while you're training? Choosing either decision-making fork is legitimate—you just need to be very clear about which fork is appropriate for this particular decision.

One of the nice things about doing an On Target model for both forks in the road is that if your situation suddenly changes, you already have your options laid out. Sometimes, when we're in a growth mode, we don't like to think about what we would do if things went wrong. We want to focus only on things going well, and yet the best time to prepare for potential problems is when things are going well.

Conversely, if you are in a survival mode, you can say, "I don't want to think about what I really want because that will just make it worse. I'll just want it more." Sometimes by looking at a growth choice you can see options you didn't know existed. Also, if you casually talk about your growth desires with people around you, you can sometimes uncover opportunities that make those growth choices possible while you are also taking care of your survival needs.

It's to your benefit to look at both angles when you're making a major decision, just as a matter of habit. You might also want to look at defining the line for you between survival and growth issues. Is survival being able to meet basic financial needs, is it emotional survival, or is it financial independence? Your definition of survival may differ from others around you—you determine what you need to meet your basic needs.

In addition, as we discussed in Chapter 1, survival and growth choices often fall along the same thematic life path (such as wanting to help others), yet survival and growth choices may seem like two divergent paths because the full-fledged growth choices happen so far down the path.

This may translate into your doing a survival-based job for a period of time that does not weave in your most important growth elements, yet allows you to save money to go back to school two years from now to pursue training in an area connected to your growth desires. By recognizing where you are along your own timeline, you can better determine the kinds of choices you need to make in the near future, and you can also keep a clear focus on the dreams and desires that your growth choices embody.

Focus on Making Smart Decisions

Looking Within

Write as many endings to each sentence as you can.

1. For me, a good decision means...

2. For me, a bad decision means...

Preparing for Your Informational Interview

Review the informational interview questions from Chapters 3 through 8. Select the questions that were most essential for you to answer and compile them into a list, ordering them from most to least important. You will want to be certain to include basic questions regarding salary, benefits, training, likelihood for advancement, and so on.

Chapter 3:

➤

➤

➤

Chapter 4:

➤

➤

➤

Chapter 5:

➤

➤

➤

Chapter 6:

➤

➤

➤

Chapter 7:

➤

➤

➤

Chapter 8:

➤

➤

➤

Additional questions:

➤

➤

➤

3. When I think about risk, I…

4. What I want most from this decision is…

Tips for a Successful Informational Interview

1. Utilize your resources. Ask family, friends, and neighbors if they can provide names of individuals working in your areas of interest.

2. Research companies, agencies, and other businesses that hire people in the fields you're considering. Call and ask for a name or names of people working in those jobs.

3. Contact the people identified in steps 1 and 2 and explain the purpose of your call:

   ➤ You currently are exploring a number of career options and want to know about the "real life" experiences of someone working in the field before you make a final decision regarding which career to pursue.

   ➤ You would like to arrange a specific time (day and length of interview) to ask some questions to increase your knowledge of the field.

   ➤ You would like to arrange the interview length, time, and location to best work with the person's schedule.

4. Prior to the interview, determine how many questions you can reasonably ask in the allotted time. Prioritize them and type up the questions with ample space between each question for writing the responses.

5. Try to jot down key phrases during the interview, rather than entire sentences. Directly after the interview, look at the key phrases you wrote down and write larger, expanded answers that reflect what you remember from the interview.

6. Arrive on time for the interview and terminate it at the agreed upon time.

7. Thank the person you interview and send a thank you note within one week of the interview. In your note, share what you found most valuable, interesting, or useful and thank the person for generously sharing his or her time and expertise with you.

Doing Your Informational Interviews

Once you've compiled your list of questions, review your updated career list from Chapter 7. Select three to five career options for which to conduct informational interviews. Call and arrange interviews, either face-to-face or by telephone. Lengthen or shorten your lists based on the time constraints of the person you're interviewing. You'll use the information you gather from these interviews when you finalize your On Target model in Chapter 10.

Consider These Questions...

1. What have you learned about your current risk threshold?

2. What helps you make satisfying decisions?

3. How might you increase the likelihood of continuing to make positive decisions?

Ideas for Action

Use this space to write down thoughts, leads, ideas, and questions that you want to pursue.

Things to explore now   *Things to explore later*

RECOMMENDED READING

Rusk, Tom. *Mind Traps.* Los Angeles: Price Stern Sloan, 1988.
Discusses 16 mind traps that create difficulties in making healthy and appropriate decisions.

Simon, Sidney. *Getting Unstuck.* New York: Time Warner, 1988.
Pinpoints ways to overcome self-imposed barriers to change and ways to take action to create a fulfilling life.

Viscott, David. *Risking.* New York: Simon and Schuster, 1977.
Assists in evaluating risks and provides a handy dos and don'ts check-list for taking reasonable risks.

10

Finding Your "Very Good Fit"

Now you're at the stage of having worked through each of the chapters, and you've had the opportunity to focus on each of the individual wedges of your On Target model. Pull out your completed On Target model, and follow along as we talk about each of the sections.

FINALIZING YOUR ON TARGET MODEL

You can proceed in two ways. You can either follow along in the book and answer the questions on your own, or you can sit down with someone you trust—a friend, a partner, a fellow student, a career counselor—and have this person ask you the questions while you look at your model and respond. Sometimes talking through this process with another person allows you to clarify and add details. If that's not possible, you might record the questions on audio tape and replay them for yourself, pausing the tape between questions to give yourself time to respond.

Let's now look at the Values wedge of your model, starting with the Very Good Fit innermost section. Ask yourself these questions:

1. What did I list as my most important values? Are there any I want to eliminate or move to another section?

2. Are there any values I might have neglected to include?

Now look at the Adequate Fit section. These are values that you would like to have as an aspect of your job but that aren't as crucial as the values you list in the innermost section of your wedge. Ask yourself these questions:

1. What did I list in this section? Do I want to eliminate or move anything to another section?

2. Are there any other values I would like to list here?

Finally, look at the Unacceptable Fit outermost section of your wedge. These are the values that you want to make certain aren't present in a job, that would cause you discomfort and disruption, and that you want to watch out for.

1. What did I list here? Is there anything I'd like to eliminate or move to another section?

2. Is there anything I'd like to add to this section?

In a similar fashion to what we've just done with the Values wedge, work your way through each section of the On Target model.

If you did survival and growth wedges for each of the areas, be sure to ask your questions for both. Make certain that you do this for each model. I think it's helpful, if you're in a classroom situation, to buddy up with a few people and share your lists. Sometimes you can listen to what someone has listed and say "Oh, how could I have forgotten to include that—that's important to me, too."

Remember, the On Target model is a snapshot of what is true for you in the moment; all the sections consist of variables related to you, and they can change and grow as you do. Your model isn't written in stone; it's written for now, to guide you in the career-change process.

When you feel you've done your best to make your model an accurate representation of what's true for you, you're ready to use it in your career-change process.

MATCHING THE MODEL TO YOUR CAREER OPTIONS

The task now, if you haven't already begun or accomplished this, is to take the information you've been gathering from the career center and informational interviews about the specifics of various jobs and begin to overlay your model with it. This could include salary, the values expressed in each job, the resources each job uses and provides, the kinds of skills required, how the job fits your notion of success, how it taps into your sense of passion and aliveness, and how it meshes with your life purpose.

Make several photocopies of your completed model. For example, if you are considering three career options, make three copies of your model. Label the top of each copy with a career option, for example, welder, dental hygienist, computer programmer.

Starting with any wedge, use highlighter pens or colored pencils to shade in whichever section of the wedge the job (for example, welder) most matches in terms of values, skills, resources and so on. Complete a shaded model for each career option.

Now, examine the shaded areas on each model. Around which section does each career option cluster—the innermost, middle, or outermost? Obviously, a career option that clusters around the innermost section signifies a better fit.

Usually, jobs zig-zag in and out of sections. If this is the case for you, you might want to prioritize your three most important wedges, those that you don't want to compromise and for which you want the fit to be as good as possible. Review your fear, worry and concern list from Chapter 2. Does anything on this list suggest which wedges you should consider most important? Now, with the models in front of you, which option makes the best sense for you? Which one is in overall alignment with your On Target model and which one is most in alignment with your top three wedges? Can you eliminate one of those three career options? You may need to gather additional information about the two remaining options or prioritize a fourth wedge in order to get additional clarity.

Refer to the decision-making discussion in Chapter 9. What kind of decision do you need to make? Are you using your correct On Target model for your present situation? If you need to make a survival-based decision, but also want to look at how these career options fit with your growth-based model, be certain that your final decision is based on the model that fits your current life circumstances.

SETTING UP TIMELINES, ACTION STEPS, AND FALL-BACK PLANS

Once you've made a decision about where you're headed in your career-change process, the next tasks are to set up your timelines, action steps, and fall-back plans. The particulars of this will vary based on whether you're jumping straight into a job search, intending to undergo a brief period of retraining, or embarking on a longer educational plan. Most community colleges have career counselors and advisors to help you through this process. Ask a counselor or someone currently in the career you're pursuing to look over your timeline and next steps to ensure that you haven't missed any details.

One of my favorite ways to set up a timeline is to make my best guess at when I need to be at the final step of my plan. For you, that might be the date you need to be hired in a new position. To set up a timeline, take several sheets of notebook paper and at the very bottom write the date your final step needs to be completed.

For example, let's say that you want to be employed by May 15. At the very bottom of the last sheet of paper, write *May 15 Start new job*. In the line above write *May 8* and the last task you need to complete before getting hired, which might be *Complete final interview and provide additional references*. Continue to work backward to the current week.

Using this approach, you choose when you need to cross the finish line and fit what you need to do into the weeks preceding it. This works well for people who procrastinate, because you put down what your next steps are each week. Often people who procrastinate do so because they feel as though there's never an end to things, especially if it's a long process. With the timeline approach, you give yourself a series of little finish lines and times to rest. Also, you can challenge yourself to get those tasks done as early as possible in the week, saying, "I've done my steps for this week. I don't have to tackle what's ahead for the next week because that's for the next week."

This approach also works well for people going back to school. If you take your entire semester or term's worth of homework, reading assignments, and papers that you need to do and break it into this format, you have to focus only on what you need to do for each week. And when you get that done, you give yourself time off, and don't force yourself to work ahead.

It's also a good idea to keep a notebook in which you list ideas that you want to incorporate into your next steps so that you don't have to carry them around in your head. You might say, "At some point, I might want to do an internship, but I don't know when I'll work it in; so I'll jot it down here." You can also use the notebook to list leads, opportunities, book suggestions, people you should talk to, and employment options.

It's also important to create fall-back plans. One way to start doing this is to make a list of the barriers that could arise in your career-change process. What could derail your process?

List of barriers:

1.

2.

3.

4.

5.

6.

7.

8.

9.

10.

Before you encounter these barriers, brainstorm what you could do to alleviate them. For example, if child care is a concern for you and if it became a problem, how might you deal with that? If you have a back injury and your injury starts to flare, what fall-back plan would allow you to continue in your process?

For each barrier you listed above, list a few fall-back plans here:

1.

2.

3.

4.

5.

6.

7.

8.

9.

10.

Only you will know where you need to safeguard yourself. It's much more productive to brainstorm fall-back plans before you need them: when you're not in a state of crisis, you can think more clearly. You can't brainstorm for a natural disaster, the death of a loved one, or many health problems. Do so for as many barriers as possible.

MOTIVATION, REWARDS, CELEBRATING EFFORT

Keeping motivated during this process is crucial, especially if you've had to push yourself through a lot of grief and fear as you've faced pursuing a new career. Find ways to cheer yourself on, and rely on supportive people in your life—those who convey their belief in you, their excitement, and their desire to support you emotionally and in more literal, practical ways.

Discover what keeps or gets you motivated. Crossing tasks off a list makes me feel as if I'm accomplishing something, and that's a motivator for me. Pinning up inspiring quotations, pictures, or anything that might represent what I'm working toward serves as a reminder and as a motivation. Consider what is most motivating to you, and experiment to determine what works for you.

Reward yourself as you move through this process, and avoid seeing the endpoint of your recareering process as your only reward. Instead, reward yourself as you're able in small- or medium-sized ways throughout the process. That might be with something as simple as a soak in a hot bath, a leisurely walk, a cup of coffee with a friend, a nap, or a good meal—whatever allows you to feel as if you're giving yourself a small reward.

Especially acknowledge that you're engaged in your career change process and that you're moving toward your goal. Sometimes you may feel you should only reward yourself for large accomplishments, yet the act of tackling the recareering process is in itself a huge accomplishment and deserves its own rewards along the way.

Celebrate your efforts. On some days you may feel, "Well, I got up, showered, got dressed and showed up for my day, but that's about all I accomplished." On those days celebrate the effort, focus, and intensity you've invested in your On Target model and your exploration of choosing a new career. Effort seems to get people places that nothing else does. Sheer effort, determination, and the act of simply showing up accomplishes an immense amount, and it's important to celebrate that as well.

I especially like creating a celebration calendar and listing on it, under the appropriate date, any events that merit celebration. If you keep that calendar for several years and continue filling it in, eventually every day becomes a reason for celebration. You can look back through it periodically and see all you've accomplished over the years, what was noteworthy and deserving of celebration.

Now you've reached the end of the book and have learned to apply your On Target model to your career-change process. Take a moment to acknowledge yourself for the motivation, self-determination, and courage it takes to tackle a project like this. I encourage you to keep this On Target model on hand for your future career changes, because you can continue to adapt this model for yourself (or other people you know may use your model as an example and a starting point for their own models). Congratulations on your current and future accomplishments and best wishes on your journey to your new career.

Index